A journalist with a diploma in international marketing, Louise Morse is currently Publicity Manager for Pilgrim Homes.

Revd Roger Hitchings was previously Director of Age Concern for Birmingham and is now a trustee of Pilgrim Homes and a pastor in the Midlands.

COULD
IT BE
DEMENTIA?

Losing your mind doesn't mean losing your soul

LOUISE MORSE
& ROGER HITCHINGS

MONARCH
BOOKS
Oxford, UK & Grand Rapids, Michigan, USA

First published in the UK in 2008 by Monarch Books
(a publishing imprint of Lion Hudson plc),
Wilkinson House, Jordan Hill Road, Oxford OX2 8DR.
Tel: +44 (0)1865 302750   Fax: +44 (0)1865 302757
Email: monarch@lionhudson.com
www.lionhudson.com

ISBN: 978-1-85424-825-1 (UK)
ISBN: 978-0-8254-6170-5 (USA)

Distributed by:
UK: Marston Book Services Ltd, PO Box 269, Abingdon, Oxon OX14 4YN;
USA: Kregel Publications, PO Box 2607, Grand Rapids, Michigan 49501

All Scripture quotations are taken from the Holy Bible, New International
Version, © 1973, 1978, 1984 by the International Bible Society. Used by
permission of Hodder & Stoughton Ltd. All rights reserved.

This book has been printed on paper and board independently certified as
having come from sustainable forests.

British Library Cataloguing Data
A catalogue record for this book is available from the British Library.

Printed and bound in Wales by Creative Print & Design.

'But if Christ is in you, your body is dead because of sin,
yet your spirit is alive because of righteousness.'
(Romans 8:10)

Contents

ACKNOWLEDGEMENTS

I doubt if it would be possible to write a book like this, which contains information from so many research centres in different countries within such a comparatively short time-scale, without the internet. My first 'thank you', then, must be to Tim Berners-Lee, the Englishman credited with making the internet possible and giving new meaning to the verb 'to browse'. Until the world-wide-web I always thought browsing was something you did in Waterstones or the Mall. Thank you, too, to the people at Netscape behind the development of the RSS (Really Simple Syndication), which I think of as a Really Simple Service and a very neat way of getting news stories delivered to my desktop every day – most major news sites have an RSS feed for much of their content.

It has been interesting to watch Alzheimer's and dementia related news stories emerge in one country and make their way, via different news services, around the world. Some stories began quite soberly, but were transmogrified in flight and ended up in the popular press with intoxicating headlines and prose promising the 'Holy Grail of discoveries', the 'major breakthrough' and suchlike.

A very big thank you is due to researchers in universities around the world who so generously share their findings on their websites. It meant I could check the facts at source. It also meant that after reading a book I could discover more about the authors and their work. Reading about Person

Centred Care is one thing, but looking at the information on Bradford University's website about the man who developed it, Professor Tom Kitwood, is quite another. He comes to life as an energetic, compassionate man who was held in affection by all who knew him. Sadly, he died in 1998, aged sixty-one, but his work is being taken forward.

My thanks too, to my reviewers: Janet Jacob, Hywel Morse, Serita Washington, Judy Mclaren, Phil Wainwright, Maureen Sim, Kim Todd, Deborah Steiner and Martin Graham, each with their own specialism, and Roger, who watched patiently as I plundered the transcripts of talks he has given over the years and responded kindly when I prodded him now and again for more. And thank you to my directors, who allowed me to almost disappear for a while to get on with the book, and publisher Tony Collins who put his foot down on further time extensions and insisted I finish it now.

I'm especially grateful to people who have first-hand knowledge of dementia and were willing to talk to me: Dr Daphne Wallace and Shirley Nurock, for example, and Christine Bryden, who took the trouble to e-mail. To all those who gave encouragement and advice – here it is! *Could it Be Dementia?* is as much yours, as it is ours.

I am delighted by this splendid book, and recommend it warmly: it opens up an important and difficult subject. I recall hearing Dr Martyn Lloyd-Jones, that great physician and pastor, say, that the Christian believer, however much disease of body or mind may later affect him, was forever 'in Christ'.

Many of us know someone who has dementia. They became forgetful and confused, and gradually we realized that their brain was failing. The media carry stories of those suffering and their poor treatment in nursing homes or hospitals: we may feel angry, but often we simply need to know more.

This book is full of carefully gathered facts and stories about Alzheimer's, and the carers of those who suffer from it. It is both challenging and comforting, facing squarely the great needs posed by dementia; it will help you with the diagnosis, show the curable causes, and examine the drugs that are now available.

Comfort comes from two sources: the unique experience of the writers in their work with the elderly and those with Alzheimer's, and the teaching given in the Bible.

We learn how the brain responds to cocoa, tea and much else, as revealed by new research. Shakespeare and the Authorized Version also help us gain understanding; perhaps by stretching the mind. But above all, beyond the wealth of facts and information, the authors reveal insight, compassion and Christian ways of showing practical care and concern. They want us to serve the elderly better, and the Gospel theme recurs: 'inasmuch as you have done it to the least of these, you have done it to Me'.

The Pilgrim Homes for which Louise Morse works started 200 years ago, and stars like Lord Shaftesbury and William Wilberforce gave their support. Would that there be many more such homes built today for Christian pilgrims nearing their journey's end. It is my hope that wealthy Christians might invest in more homes for the elderly.

I recall many elderly Christians who have influenced me: they reflected God's grace in a special way, with ripe wisdom and humour. This book may help us to do more to help them 'finish their course with joy'. I hope it will be enjoyed by many, and used as a resource by Christians and churches everywhere.

Dr Gaius Davies
Emeritus Consultant Psychiatrist

Why we have put dementia in a Christian context

Much factual information is available about dementia, but there is little from a Christian perspective. Yet dementia can raise questions for Christians unlike any other condition. Why does a godly old man begin to use language that has always been anathema to him? Why does a loving mother become stubborn and suspicious? What is happening to a beloved husband, who is behaving as though he never knew you? Above all, where is God in all of this? Our aim in writing *Could it Be Dementia?* is to give as much practical information as we can, and to restore a sense of divine purpose where this has been lost.

Dementia is a Latin word that means, literally, apart from, or away from the mind. It is one of the least understood of conditions, and one of the most feared. It seems to hold the place that cancer did forty years ago. In 1961, 90 per cent of doctors said they would prefer not to tell cancer patients their diagnosis. By 1977 that opinion had been completely reversed, with 97 per cent of doctors then in favour of disclosing. The reasons for silence in 1961 were similar to those now given with Alzheimer's (a major cause of dementia) – there was no cure. Now there are cures for cancer, along with treatments that extend patients' lives, and determined researchers are working to ensure that this will eventually be the case with Alzheimer's and other forms of dementia. In the meantime, it is so dreaded that two-thirds of people researched said they would not want a diagnosis of Alzheimer's to be disclosed to their relatives, although, interestingly, two-thirds said that if it were their diagnosis, they would prefer to know.

Dementia stretches our resources and tests our faith, and it needs to be put into a Christian context. And what a rich context that is! Even before we were born, God knew every detail of our lives. Our view stretches from before the world was formed, to the grave and beyond – to the *real* life that never ends; past these 'shadowlands' (as C.S. Lewis described life on earth) to the glorious 'uplands' with Jesus Christ. We are not left to struggle on our own until we arrive there because God has 'set His seal of ownership on us, and put His Spirit in our hearts as a deposit, guaranteeing what is to come' (2 Corinthians 1:22). Christianity is not just intellectual assent to a set of principles or a code of belief – it is a profound transaction that takes place when we accept Christ as our Saviour.

The core content of this book was planned originally as a series of leaflets to help the residents of Pilgrim Homes and others. But, increasingly, wherever our managers and supporters have taken seminars, or given talks about caring for elderly Christians, the most pressing need has been for information and reassurance about dementia.

Pilgrim Homes was founded as 'The Aged Pilgrims' Friend Society' in 1807. Initially the Charity helped with reliable pensions (long before the welfare state!), and practical gifts such as coal, food, and blankets; but always with spiritual support. Nowadays we care for elderly Christians with sheltered housing, and residential and nursing homes. Our schemes are renowned for their Christian ethos and loving care.

Contrary to common belief, in later years Christians need more spiritual support than at any time in their lives: even those who have been faith leaders or missionaries. For old age is a time of loss – loss of physical and mental ability, and of trust, even in one's own judgment. Satan reserves his fiercest attacks for God's elderly saints. As well as our staff, groups of supporters from local churches befriend our residents, and encourage them in their faith. These supporters also pray for the management teams and carers, and provide speakers for services in the homes.

Perhaps the greatest encouragement, for residents and carers alike, is seeing the Holy Spirit at work in His people. In a worship meeting, someone who normally does not speak will unexpectedly pray the most cogent, appropriate prayer; another will sing a chorus – word-perfect; another will say something that only the Holy Spirit could have revealed. Residents who usually pay little attention to what is said to them will fasten their attention on a visiting pastor for the duration of his preaching. As residents join in Grace before mealtimes, carers say they see an almost tangible atmosphere of calm and comfort descend. In countless other ways the Holy Spirit is seen to be present with God's precious 'aged pilgrims'.

Much of this book is based on talks given to our staff by Pastor Roger Hitchings. He is referred to throughout as 'Roger'. Before he became a pastor, Roger was a director with Age Concern in Birmingham, managing the largest Day Unit for Alzheimer's sufferers in the UK. He and his wife also managed a care home. Roger's mother developed dementia, and died in one of our care homes. He is also one of Pilgrim Homes' trustees. I worked as a journalist and broadcaster in the Middle East, and later ran a public relations agency in Cambridge, helping companies with their marketing communications. For several years now, I have worked for Pilgrim Homes on a range of communications, both internal and external.

One of the most delightful aspects of my job is talking to carers and residents, and I am inspired by their lives and their 'proven characters' (Romans 5:3–4, NASB). The very first resident I interviewed was a white-haired, ninety-year-old lady who was translating the Old Testament into the dialect of the region in India where she had been a missionary for forty years. In agreeing to let me write the article, she told me firmly, 'This must not be about me but for the glory of God.' Quietly spoken and very simply dressed, she exuded graciousness and a sense of royalty.

As the number of people with dementia increases, more and more church fellowships will be affected. It is both a challenge and a marvellous opportunity. Referring to how Christians helped each other nearly two thousand years ago, Tertullian of Carthage, a prominent Roman Christian, was able to write, 'This is why people say of us, "See, how these Christians love one another!"' (see John 13:35). It would be wonderful if, observing how Christian fellowships respond to families affected by dementia, people could say the same thing about us, today.

Jesus said, 'If you give a cup of water in My name...' and 'what you do to them, you do to Me' (see Matthew 10:42; 25:40). We hope that in a small way this book will help to bring a 'cup of water' to someone whose life has been changed by dementia.

CHAPTER 1

Finding Wonders in the Dark

'Are Your wonders known in the place of darkness, or Your righteous deeds in the land of oblivion?'
(Psalm 88:12)

A despairing wife said, 'Every morning I wake up and look over and see Jack, and think of our long life together. I think how much I love him. Then he wakes up, and it's not Jack.' Nancy Reagan, the wife of the former US President, famously described his ten years with dementia as 'the long goodbye'. Someone else has said of caring for someone with dementia, 'Two of you make the journey together, but only one of you comes back.'

It can be heartbreaking for relatives to watch the progress of dementia, as the person seems to disappear and only the physical shell remains. Dementia is often called a family disease, because the stress of watching a loved one slowly decline affects everyone. And the incidence of dementia is rising so quickly that almost everyone you meet knows someone who is suffering from it. The statistics are mind-boggling.

Every year there are 4.6 million new cases of dementia – the equivalent of one new case of dementia every seven seconds.[1] Worldwide there are currently 24 million people suffering from dementia, and over the next thirty-four years that number will increase to 81 million.[2] On an international scale, that amounts to 1,676,471 cases diagnosed a year: around 190 people an hour. In America[3] the number of people affected by dementia is expected to increase three fold in the next fifty years, from 4 million in 2007 to a total of more than 13 million. In Australia, the 2006 estimated prevalence of dementia is 1.03 per cent of the population as a whole. In the UK, at the time of writing (2007) there are around 684,000 people with dementia, and that figure is expected to rise to 940,110 by 2021, and 1,735,087 by 2051, an increase of 38 per cent over the next fifteen years and 154 per cent over the next forty-five years. It is not a new disease, but one that has been thrown into sharp relief by the rise in the number of sufferers in an increasingly ageing population. Although it affects mainly older people, there are also around eight thousand people under the age of sixty-five with dementia in the UK. It is not an inevitable part of ageing, and not everyone will develop it, but everyone will be affected by it, in one way or another.

Dementia affects one in five people over the age of sixty-five and one in four over the age of eighty, and according to government predictions, there will be 4 million people aged over eighty-five by 2051. Among them are likely to be a large number of practising Christians, for research shows that 'people with a faith, who regularly attend a place of worship' tend to live longer than their peers. Much excellent information about dementia is produced by organizations such as the Alzheimers' Disease Society, Age Concern, Help the Aged and others, but it is factual, and has no spiritual context. Yet Christians have a glorious context in which to put this dreadful disease, a context which steadies us in the present and balances us in the light of eternity.

Dementia is a Latin word that means, literally, apart from, or away from the mind. It is an umbrella term used to describe the loss of cognitive or intellectual function. It is not a disease, but a group of symptoms that may accompany some diseases or conditions affecting the brain.

Every person on earth will leave this life at some point. I've heard people say that when their time comes they would like to die peacefully in their sleep, or go suddenly with an unsuspected illness. If we could choose the way we leave this life, I doubt anyone would choose dementia. The fear it arouses, and the pain it leaves, can be devastating. I had no real idea how deep its effects can be until I began to arrange a seminar on caring for the elderly at a national Christian conference. My contact in the host organization was a lady in her mid-thirties whose mother had only recently been diagnosed with dementia. She said, 'You don't get it till it hits you! We're losing our mother, my sister and I, and suddenly we've become the parents. And we don't understand what's going on, or the best thing to do.' As an afterthought she asked, 'Are older people always so stubborn? Is it something that comes when you get older?' Because her story was so typical we agreed that I would interview her as part of the introduction to the dementia segment of the seminar, but in the event she left the hall in tears before I could talk to her. I learnt more than I expected from the audience at this seminar, and their comments and questions gave impetus to the writing of this book.

Although Pilgrim Homes has been caring for elderly

Christians of every Protestant denomination for 200 years, it was almost unknown at this conference – the annual conference of the Assemblies of God. It was only the second year we had attended. It was the first time we had organized a seminar there, so we were pleased and surprised to see so many delegates turn up for it. When we began to talk about dementia there were sad faces and tears, along with some audible punctuation, which I put down to the fact that this was a more expressive denomination than most. But it was the intense body language and facial expression of one listener that really caught my eye. He was probably in his early fifties, with a stocky frame, broad cheekbones, and a face set in the lines of a habitual listener. He also had an indefinable air of responsibility and authority, and I mentally ticked him as a pastor. He sat like a coiled spring, leaning forward and listening with a fierce concentration. I kept a wary eye on him because I thought he might be gearing up to ask difficult denominational-type questions (Pilgrim Homes is undenominational), but when we opened up the session later for questions and comments he left, making no comment. After the seminar, a number of people came to our stand for extra copies of the notes to take back to their churches, and I didn't see him again until the next day, when he came along just before lunch.

Unaware of the impression he had made the morning before, he introduced himself by saying he had been to the seminar. Then he paused, seeming to gather himself before saying intently, 'I never got over what happened to my grandma... I never got over it.'

There was no need to tell me that she had died with dementia, and no need to explain the process or the pain. The exhibition seemed to disappear and we were caught up in a conversation without words, just speaking with our eyes: his deeply grieving, mine empathizing. We stood in silence for a moment. Some communications are better without words (as Job's friends illustrate so well), but sometimes they are expected and needed – and they have to be the right ones.

I thought, not for the first time, how important it is to remind ourselves of what we know but can forget in times of grief and strain – that God is not some distant aspiration but actually lives in us (John 14:17) and has said He will never leave us (Hebrews 13:5). He has promised that nothing will separate us from Him and His love; nothing, not even dementia. So I said how blessed he was to have had such a loving grandma in the first place, and (knowing that she could not have been anything other than a Lois to this Timothy) we both knew she was all right, now. I reminded him that all the time she had had dementia and perhaps couldn't communicate with anybody, the Holy Spirit was right there with her, communicating and comforting in ways we can't see.

'You might not have been able to see your grandma any more, but she was still there all right, and *he* did,' I said.

He nodded. He already knew this, of course, but sometimes we need to hear what we know, as affirmation, from others.

The light may be off, but someone is in

I told him of the times in our care homes when, like lightning flashes through darkness, there are fleeting moments of grace; glimpses when the person with dementia breaks through and is seen again.

During a chapel service at our Wellsborough home, the

manager noticed a resident, who is not normally able to remember very much at all, singing the chorus to a hymn, word-perfect and with her face aglow, lifted upwards. When the chorus began again, he looked to see if the same thing would happen, and sure enough, eyes shut again and face lifted, she was singing the words, 'O make me understand it, help me to take it in, what it meant to Thee the Holy One to bear away my sin.' During conversation afterwards, he asked if she enjoyed the singing and which hymn meant the most to her, but she could not remember the hymns or singing the chorus.

In another of our homes I had a perfectly ordinary conversation lasting for about twenty minutes with one of our volunteer home visitors and a resident, discussing her life before she came into the home, why she felt she had to come in, how she had managed to get a place when it was then quite full, and what she thought of living there.

As we left the room, the home visitor turned to me in amazement and said, 'That is the most lucid Elsie has been for the past two years. She's normally very confused.'

Unlocking confused minds

Philip Grist, a pastor who preaches regularly in our care homes, tells of an experience that radically changed his attitude towards preaching to God's elderly children. He said, 'A resident had severe Alzheimer's disease. She possessed a very sweet nature and a lovely smile, but could speak only two or three words. She sat quietly in her chair, mouth open wide and with a completely vacant look. On one occasion, as I gave out my text, her mouth closed, her eyes came alive and were riveted to me the whole time I was preaching. When I concluded, the vacant look returned and her mouth immediately dropped open. Nothing was clearer to me than that the Holy Spirit had communicated the Word of God to the soul of that saint.' He saw how, as the Holy Spirit can unlock the hearts of lifeless sinners, in the same way He can unlock the confused minds of His elderly people. We see this in the prayers that dementia sufferers sometimes unexpectedly say.

Ruth, a manager of one of our largest homes, thinks that the fact that a sufferer can offer up a meaningful prayer at exactly the right moment is one of the strongest proofs that God exists. Far from being a thoughtless repetition of things learned long ago, these prayers are fresh and appropriate.

Dorothy Moran is retired now, and spends a day each week helping to run a day care programme for residents with dementia. She says they have taught her so much over the years, and she is still learning. She recalls an occasion when, after a showing of missionary slides, the meeting was opened to prayer. The first person to pray was a gentleman who could barely string two words together in everyday conversation. He prayed a relevant and moving prayer, having clearly understood a great deal of what he had seen and heard. His spirit was alive and well.

Dorothy said, 'Two staff members and I keep one day a week especially for up to eight residents who are living with dementia. This is a day filled with joy and laughter, fun and games, food and fellowship. The other day a visitor said, "You all sounded to be having such fun in there I nearly came in and joined you!" Sometimes other staff members will bring their cups of tea and join us for a little while.

'It brings such joy when someone who rarely moves manages to catch and throw a ball, another who rarely speaks adds a few words to the conversation, another who has difficulty eating enjoys a good dinner and clears the plate, another reads a hymn or a psalm, or leads in prayer. Sometimes we notice two participants holding an animated "conversation", which may not be understandable to us, but they are obviously enjoying it. These dear people have taught me so much over the years and I am still learning! I can answer yes, the darkness can speak of miracles, and yes, there are treasures hidden in the darkness.'

Throughout the coming chapters we will be looking at dementia the Pilgrim way. We will see what it is and what it is not; the care and resources available; how to prepare if you are diagnosed with dementia yourself; ways of helping sufferers and carers; strategies when visiting; and coping in the community and fellowships. We will be putting it into the context of eternity; looking at it through Christian eyes and seeing through the darkness to the treasure hidden there.

CHAPTER 2

Where is the Real Me?

'Now we know that if the earthly tent we live in is
destroyed, we have a building from God, an eternal house
in heaven, not built by human hands. ...
Now it is God who has made us for this very purpose and
has given us the Spirit as a deposit,
guaranteeing what is to come.'
(2 Corinthians 5:1, 5)

Sometimes we need reminding that, as Christians, we take a
different view of life to people around us. We carry within us
a sense of eternity and separateness, even though we are not
fully conscious of it most of the time. We are pilgrims on our
way Home. It is our magnetic north, and our 'inner person'
is being constantly drawn to it. The more treasure we have
there, the stronger the pull.

We see this every day with our elderly residents, many of
whom have more family and friends in heaven than on earth,
and talking with them can be a delight. It is as if they can
almost see the Celestial City; can smell the healing leaves on
the trees and hear the sound of singing. It can make them
long to discard their aching old bones and be off. Even
though they are dearly loved by our staff, sometimes they

will say in no uncertain terms that they want to enter those gates sooner, rather than later.

'Why doesn't the Lord come and take me now?' one frail, illness-free 103-year-old asked the home manager. 'What is He waiting for?'

A Dutch friend told of an elderly aunt who, in the weeks before she died, asked her more than once, 'What is this Easter music I am hearing?'

Someone with a very strong magnetic pull is Winifred, a delightful 86-year-old former nurse who cared virtually single-handedly for her husband for over thirty years. He had been diagnosed in his early fifties with a degenerative disease that gradually paralysed him. Winifred coped magnificently until her early eighties, when they both realized she did not have the strength to carry on. After some determined searching for a Christian care home, they came to live in one of ours, and Winifred and her husband enjoyed twenty blissful weeks there until he died. Afterwards, although she was fit enough to live on her own, she decided to stay on in the home. Her purpose now, she felt, was to help with the other residents, most of who are much frailer.

'I can't tell you how happy I was when the staff here said they would let me help,' she told me.

She doesn't help in a physical or official way, but she is a source of encouragement and joy to everyone. Not long after her husband's death, she lost a daughter to cancer, leaving Winifred the sole survivor of her natural family. When I met her some weeks later there was sadness but no sense of deep grieving or of irreparable loss.

Around the same time my eight-year-old grandson had died of a rare genetic disorder and, after a few minutes' commiserating with each other, Winifred said simply, 'Now we have even more links with the Homeland.'

More often than not, we are so caught up in the sheer challenge of living that we forget who we really are. Some years ago a journalist and I were discussing, over coffee, a news story about the extreme lengths some women were going to, with plastic surgery and gruelling diets, to make themselves attractive. Thinking of my overweight, pear-shaped self, I said that I was glad I wasn't just my body, but that I simply lived in it.

She snapped back, 'That's not true – that's faith talking.'

She was right, it was faith talking; however, she was also wrong, because the Bible makes it clear that we are 'tent-dwellers', living in temporary accommodation. (2 Corinthians 5:4). When we see the lights of Home more clearly and these tents are worn with age, we want to put them off, and put on the real thing (1 Corinthians 15:53).

Looking for the inner self

If we are living in these 'tents' for the time being, and our brains are a physical part of them, where are *we*, actually? Is our inner self, the essence of the person, simply the result of the brain structure we were born with? Philosophers searched for centuries to find the 'seat of the soul'. The French philosopher Descartes thought that it was in a portion of the brain, the pineal gland. Psychology has determinedly divided itself from philosophy, but the question still dogs psychologists. John Gabrieli, Associate Professor of Psychology at Stanford University, asks, 'What we are wondering is, where does personality come from?'[1] It also intrigues neurologists. Widely reported in the media in late 1997, was a paper entitled The Neural Basis of Religious Experience given at the annual meeting of the Society for

Neuroscience by Dr Vilayanur Ramachandran, a neuroscientist at the University of California, San Diego. The implications were that there may be dedicated neural 'machinery' in our brains concerned with religion, and that, we, as a species, are genetically programmed to believe in God. Now there's a surprise, I thought, as I read the summary on the internet.[2] It put me in mind of Sir Francis Crick's warning in his autobiography that 'biologists must constantly keep in mind that what they see was not designed, but rather evolved.' Could it be that they need this reminder because, as Professor Richard Dawkins said in his book *The Blind Watchmaker*, 'living things overwhelmingly impress us with the appearance of design as if by a master watchmaker'?[3] God made human beings in His own image, the Bible tells us, and in such a way that He can communicate with us and enjoy our company. We know from the Scriptures and from the Holy Spirit within us that we are much more than simply the sum of our parts.

We know, too, that the way we communicate and project ourselves to others is enabled by different parts of the brain. When it is damaged, either by disease or injury, the personality can seem to be radically changed. One of the saddest accounts I ever read was of a man who had sustained brain injuries in a car crash. As he regained consciousness he tried to twist his head off, crying out, 'Take it off me! I've got the wrong head!'

With today's sophisticated equipment scientists can watch the brain at work, seeing parts of it 'light up' as it carries out different tasks. They can obtain different reactions by stimulating parts of it, with probes or drugs. One of the world's foremost imaging research facilities is the Wellcome Trust Centre for Neuro-imaging at University College

London (UCL). Some years ago a study the Centre did with London cab drivers showed that they had enlarged a part of their brain, the hippocampus, by acquiring the 'knowledge', an extensive period of learning the map of the city, and by constantly having to navigate its maze of streets. It is interesting to note that the cabbies' abilities were not dictated by their brains, but their brains, or at least this part of them, were shaped by their environment and behaviour. Their brain structure did not dictate their choice of behaviour, but responded to it. The ability of the brain to change with learning is what is known as neuroplasticity.[4] As well its genetic inheritance, the brain is shaped by the characteristics of a person's environment and by the actions of that same person.

In this connection, an interesting study on the brains of violent criminals was undertaken a few years ago. Researchers found that many of them had a smaller than normal amygdala, the almond-shaped part of the brain that handles emotions. A British television programme hypothesized that the criminals were themselves victims of a deficient brain structure and should be treated accordingly, an interpretation which seemed to ignore the notion of neuroplasticity. But I have not read of anyone presenting a smaller than normal amygdala in court as a defence.

'I am fearfully and wonderfully made; Your works are wonderful, I know that full well', wrote the psalmist (139:14). Musing on how God knew everything about him, even understanding his thoughts and anticipating his words, he wrote, 'Such knowledge is too wonderful for me, too lofty for me to attain' (Psalm 139:6).

If our personalities were the result, in part or in whole, of the brain we genetically inherit then, when the brain died, so would we. It would be 'lights out' for us: the end. But if, as Jesus Christ promised, there is life after physical death and, by the sound of it, a better life than most people currently enjoy, then the assumption is that our brains, like the rest of our bodies, are the controls that we use that help us express ourselves and interact with the physical world. As we are unable to see heaven with our physical eyes, so we are unable to see the real 'us', despite science's most advanced tools. The Bible tells us that 'The body that is sown is perishable, it is raised imperishable; it is sown in dishonour, it is raised in glory; it is sown in weakness, it is raised in power; it is sown a natural body, it is raised a spiritual body' (1 Corinthians 15:42–44). This is a promise God has made. It means that the pastor I met at the conference will once again worship with his grandma. Jack and his wife will hold a conversation again. They will each have a new body, perfectly suited to heaven. We can understand the part 'sown in weakness ... sown a natural body', because we feel it and we see it. We cannot describe our new, spiritual bodies (though I have heard a few preachers give their ideas), but we have a sense of it in our spirits, like the smell of coffee before it is poured. The Spirit of God within us sketches it on our souls, because, as 2 Corinthians 1:22 assures us, He has 'set His seal of ownership on us, and put His Spirit in our hearts as a deposit, guaranteeing what is to come.' How kind of God, to give us a foretaste of Glory!

CHAPTER 3

The Thief that Comes to Destroy

'For the perishable must clothe itself with the
imperishable, and the mortal with immortality.'
(1 Corinthians 15:53)

The normal adult human brain typically weighs between
1 and 1.5 kg (2–3 lb) and has an average volume of 1.6 litres.[1]
The mature human brain consumes some 20–25 per cent of
the energy used by the body, and is arguably the most important part of the anatomy. This small mass of spongy pinky-
grey matter consists of more than 100 billion neurons, or
nerve cells. Dementia is caused by the loss of functioning
neurons as a result of changes that occur in the brain. It is
like a thief that sneaks onto the bridge and destroys the controls, resulting inexorably in shipwreck. In this chapter we
look at the various ways that this thief gains entry. It is an
overview gleaned from reports in the media and checked
with research centres' websites. Universities and researchers
are generous with their information, but I need to stress that
this is a reportage – a body of reported news – and not an
expert appraisal.

The most common cause, accounting for 58 per cent of cases of dementia, is Alzheimer's disease, named after the German neurologist who described it 100 years ago; followed by vascular disease, dementia with Lewy bodies, frontotemporal dementia (including Pick's disease), alcohol-related dementia (including Korsakoff's syndrome), and AIDS-related dementia. The Alzheimer's Society website (www.alzheimers.org.uk) is an excellent source of reference about the most common causes. There is no known cure or preventative treatment, or even a sure and certain diagnosis except at autopsy, although scientists are developing blood tests, examining proteins in spinal fluid, and developing dyes that work with brain imaging techniques. The most sophisticated tests are emerging in North America, but as a Suffolk GP commented, 'We're not likely to see them here on the NHS for some time.' (The National Health Service (NHS) is Britain's state-run health system.)

From the number of studies that have been published, it seems that the bulk of dementia research is directed at the major cause, Alzheimer's disease, although this may be because the Alzheimer's Society is very good at disseminating information. Very little has been discovered since Alzheimer first described the disease over 100 years ago, and the progress being made recently is probably due to today's rapidly improving technology. It was the same in Alzheimer's day: the findings on his patient's brain at autopsy which led to the definition of the disease were possible because of new advances in microscopy and a method of silver staining of histological sections (slices of dead tissue) introduced by a colleague, Franz Nissl.

Over the previous five years, one of Alzheimer's patients had become increasingly anxious and disoriented, apathetic and unable to care for herself. She told him at one point, 'I have lost myself.' The autopsy revealed extensive plaques and tangles in her brain.

When Alzheimer elucidated it at a medical meeting, it was the first time that the symptoms and the pathology of the disease were presented together. Hundreds, or probably thousands, of autopsies since then have confirmed the existence of these plaques and tangles, more properly known as beta-amyloid and tau, a protein that gets transformed in such a way that strands of it stick together like cold pasta.

Millions of pounds are being spent on research to come up with a drug that will prevent these plaques and tangles in the first place, or halt their development in the second, and the first researchers to come up with the answers will probably be as famous as Crick and Watson, the scientists who first described the structure of DNA. However, laboratory breakthroughs are coming in quickly. In August 2007 researchers at the University of St Andrews said they had found a way to create a synthetic substance which can impede a process in nerve cells which would otherwise produce symptoms of dementia. Moreover, in tests, the compound reversed damage that had already been done to cognitive function, memory and learning ability. Dr Frank Gunn-Moore,[2] senior lecturer at St Andrews' School of Biology, said: 'We have shown that it is possible to reverse some of the signs associated with Alzheimer's disease.' The work is now being continued to try and refine the inhibitor into a potential drug with no toxic or deleterious side effects.

Finding the cause

The answer to the dilemma might, in fact, lie in our DNA. Most of the global research so far seems to lean to a genetic predisposition, although there is no single gene for

Alzheimer's disease, and inherited factors alone do not explain why some people develop it while others do not. An Australian study found that a gene (AP0E4) associated with Alzheimer's disease becomes active only in old age, and has no effect on cognition until then – and even then, not every elderly person is affected. Researchers at the Albert Einstein College of Medicine at Yeshiva University[3] studied 158 people who lived to 95 or beyond. They found that those who inherited a particular version of a gene known as CETP were twice as likely to have a sharp and alert brain when they are elderly. They were also five times less likely than people with a different version of the same gene to develop Alzheimer's disease and other forms of dementia.

A team of scientists from the University of British Columbia in Vancouver, Canada is reported to have proved that illnesses which reduce blood flow (and thereby oxygen to the brain), including strokes and heart attacks, are likely to lead to the sufferer developing Alzheimer's. The link between oxygen and plaque formation is thought to be a gene called BACE 1, and in studies with mice this gene's activity increased when it was denied a regular supply of oxygen. Team leader Mr Weihong Song explained: 'If you have less oxygen, you turn up this gene and obviously generate more beta-amyloid. If you have a higher level of beta-amyloid, you form more plaque, if you have this plaque, then you will have dementia.'

The research led Professor Clive Ballard, Director of Research at the Alzheimer's Society, to say that regular exercise could help prevent dementia because it provides the brain with a regular supply of fresh blood.

The importance of a good blood supply to the brain was emphasized in a research paper published by the University of Rochester Medical Centre in the *Proceedings of the National Academy of Sciences* in January 2007. Neuroscientists and cardiovascular experts collaborating over a five year period found that, while the first apparent symptom of Alzheimer's may be a person forgetting names or faces, the very first physical change is actually a decline in the amount of blood that flows in the brain. Two dominant proteins, myocardin and SRF (serum response factor), known for the control they exert on blood vessel walls, are implicated. Using today's best imaging technologies, the experts found that not only is blood flow within the brain reduced, but the body's capacity to allocate blood to different areas of the brain on demand is blunted in people with the disease.

Professor Berislav Zlokovic, a neurovascular expert heading the team noted, 'A reduction in blood flow precedes the decline in cognitive function in Alzheimer's patients.' It is a sense of back to basics, because although Alzheimer noted changes both in the brain's cells and in the small arteries and capillaries that supply and drain blood to and from the brain, over the decades the changes to blood vessels have been pushed to the background as researchers separated the two concepts and focused mainly on the toxic effects of the disease on cells. Now, Professor Zlokovic said, 'More and more, people are paying attention to the role of the vascular system in Alzheimer's disease.'

Support for this view comes from research at the Leiden University Medical Center in the Netherlands. Using magnetic resonance imaging, researchers measured the average total blood flow to the brains of elderly patients with and without dementia, and a control group of healthy young people. The flow to younger people was 742 millilitres per minute; in older people without dementia it was 551 ml per minute, in those with dementia it was an average of 443 ml a minute.

These studies are among many that are examining pathologies other than beta-amyloid and plaques. They question whether these plaques and tangles are the causes of the dementia observed by Alzheimer or the result of a real, 'upstream' culprit. They could be simply like a scab on your knee, a response to an earlier injury. Others are investigating the way diabetes affects the brain; for example, a dysfunction in the way brain cells of a certain genetic stripe use glucose may lead to the destruction of dendrites, the neuron's main way to communicate. 'There is more to Alzheimer's than B-amyloid alone' was the conclusion of an Alzheimer's research roundtable reported in the *Alzheimer's & Dementia* journal in October 2006.

Alzheimer's is the most common cause of dementia and seems to attract the most publicity, but it is not the only one. Frontotemporal dementia (FTD) is not so well known to the public, yet it is said to be the most common form of dementia in people under the age of sixty-five, typically striking between the ages of forty and sixty-four. Like Alzheimer's, it is characterized by abnormal deposits of proteins in the brain.

Vascular dementia describes all those forms caused by damage to the blood vessels leading to the brain. Symptoms of vascular dementia can happen either suddenly, following a stroke, or over time, through a series of small strokes in the brain, causing 'multi-infarct dementia'. The most common condition is thought to be a combination of both Alzheimer's and vascular dementia.[4] There is a good deal of advice in the literature, in this connection, about treating raised blood pressure and high cholesterol levels and exercising regularly, and we look at the measures we are told we can sensibly take to avoid developing dementia in chapter 6.

Dementia with Lewy bodies gets its name from the tiny spherical structures made of proteins that develop inside nerve cells. Their presence in the brain leads to the degeneration and death of brain tissue, affecting memory, concentration and language skills. People with dementia with Lewy bodies may have visual hallucinations, and may also develop physical problems such as slowness of movement, stiffness and tremor.

There are other less common causes of dementia, including Pick's disease, where damage is more localized than in Alzheimer's disease, usually beginning in the frontal lobe of the brain. Dementia can also be caused by the effect of toxins: for example, Korsakoff's syndrome is caused by alcohol abuse, again with damage specific to the frontal lobes of the brain.

Not good if detached

One of the severest, most devastating Korsakoff's syndrome cases was observed by neurologist Dr Oliver Sacks. In his book *The Man Who Mistook His Wife for a Hat*, Dr Sacks tells of Jimmie, a man who had dense amnesia and could not remember isolated items for more than a few seconds. Everyone concerned with his care had an overwhelming sense of something missing, and Dr Sacks wondered if he had lost the essence of himself; if he was a spiritual casualty, a 'lost soul'. He put this to one of the Sisters, who suggested he observe Jimmie during a service in the hospital chapel. There he saw him worshipping, 'no longer at the mercy of a faulty and fallible mechanism – that of meaningless sequences and memory traces – absorbed in an act of his whole being, which carried feeling and meaning in an organic continuity and unity, a continuity and unity so seamless it could not permit any break'.[5] Jimmie had led a chaotic and increasingly isolated life, and for him that sense of continuity and unity came late. But better late than never.

For me, Jimmie's story is a lovely illustration of the Lord's tenacity. God made us for unity and continuity, with Him and with each other. 'Not good if detached' is as true of our souls as it is of the controls of the bridge of our ship. This seems to be confirmed by research published in February 2007 in the American Archives of General Psychiatry by Rush University's Alzheimer's Disease Center in Chicago[6] which showed that a sense of connectedness might help prevent dementia, while the opposite – isolation and loneliness – could increase the risk of developing it. These findings have huge implications for older people, most of whom, for a number of reasons, have fewer social contacts than those in younger age groups. The way our society is fragmenting does not make it look any better for the future.

When I was growing up, I knew the people who lived in every house on my street. I used to run errands for some of them. They were unofficial policemen, keeping an eye on us children and reporting serious escapades to our parents. I never understood why my tip-toeing over the ornamental spikes of the 12 ft high school gate was any business of the neighbour who spotted me from her kitchen window fifty yards away, but that was not the point. They were there, seeing what went on, and that included 'looking out' for older people. But those small, close communities do not exist anymore, at least not in the towns and cities where most of us live. 'Modern life has severed the connections that once gave it meaning,' observes author Maeve Haran in an article, 'How to be truly happy', in *The Daily Telegraph*; 'the everyday pleasures that bring most happiness, it seems to me, lie in connectedness. We no longer live in the place where we were born. We travel everywhere by car, shop in anonymous supermarkets and often hardly know our neighbours. No wonder we sometimes feel depressed or isolated.' Ms Haran renewed her sense of connectedness by getting to know the people in her neighbourhood, simply speaking to them and finding out a little bit about them – the history of the local wine store, and others.

It's the small touches that make connections, and they are mostly up to us. It takes hardly any effort to say 'Hello' or get to know people in your everyday life. I think God also enjoys our small touches during the day, as well as the longer, more contemplative time we spend with Him. It's acknowledging His Spirit within us, and developing a natural dialogue. I remember listening to an evangelist preaching on this topic of developing a real, close relationship with God, and saying, 'You have asked Jesus Christ into your heart and into your life. He is more than an honoured, temporary Guest. He wants to share your life with you.' Then he asked, 'Would you ask someone to share your life and only spend time with him on certain, special occasions? No – you would talk to each other.'

I saw a lovely example of this living connection some years ago, in an American magazine. There was a small poem written by an older man which went something like

Hey God! Just look at that sunset over there! Look
how it's going down over the trees, setting the leaves

on fire! Look at the long shadows it's sending up the road. What a fantastic world You've made! I'd like to jig a few little steps right here, and maybe hop and skip a bit up the road, but those folks on the bus might think me somewhat strange. So I'll just tip my hat and say, 'evening'; but hey God – look at that sunset!

Connections are important. I had gone into a 'Buy-Low' store in South Carolina to buy some coffee and, as always, got taken up with how different products on sale there were from those in England. I couldn't find the coffee, so asked a man who was replenishing some of the shelves where it was. He told me it was three aisles along, and I went over to find it. A moment later he appeared around the corner of the aisle.

'Ma'am,' he said, 'I couldn't help notice you have an accent.'

'I'm from England,' I replied. (It's far too much trouble to say the United Kingdom or Great Britain overseas, because you're always 'from England', even if you live in the tip of Scotland or in South Wales.)

'Could I ask you, ma'am, how you got here?'

'Well, I flew American Airlines from London,' I answered, puzzled.

'Ma'am, could I ask you if you believe in Jesus Christ?' he responded.

'If I didn't believe in Jesus Christ, I wouldn't fly at all!' I told him.

Then I understood. He was looking for an opportunity to evangelize, and was searching for a point of connection. We stood and fellowshipped for a minute or two, and both our days were blessed. It doesn't take much to stay connected.

CHAPTER 4

The Importance of Belonging

'So in Christ we who are many form one body,
and each member belongs to all the others.'
(Romans 12:5)

A popular song some years ago began, 'People who need people'. When I heard it, I wondered, 'Who doesn't need people?'

At the tip of God's creation are people. We are made in His own image, and the relationship enjoyed by the Father, the Son and the Holy Spirit shows us that God made people for people. God himself is a relational being. We need relationships with other people. If we don't have them, we don't progress as human beings. Of all the people in the world, Christians should have the healthiest relationships, because we belong to a beautiful family with relatives near and far, from the far corners of the globe to the local church.

In my church, after the Sunday morning service we amble to a room at the back where tea and coffee (and sometimes Welsh cakes) are served. There are conveniently placed chairs for the older folk and the children help themselves to cake, or cookies, or bake-stones (as Welsh cakes used to be called). It isn't that we need refreshments, because everyone seems to live quite close to the church and could be making their own in a very short time. We are interested in each other, we want to talk – to find out how we all are and what's happening in each other's worlds. We take home things to think about and to pray for. We have different lives but common values, and a blood tie that links us more deeply than perhaps we realize. Is there anything like the local church where people can come together week after week, in such a natural way?

These connections are vital, because it is not an easy thing to be an older person in today's world. It is becoming an increasingly impersonal place. Technology has made this an age of easy communication, but increasing depersonalization. Technology means that my gas meter can tell my supplier how much I have used, but to speak to the gas company, or any other service provider, I am led through several impersonal electronic gateways. One hotel company even uses a digitized voice that asks questions like a robot and waits for a verbal response. It is like being passed through the eye of a needle. By the time my call is answered by a real, live person I feel that parts of my individuality have been scraped away, like the travellers' baggage in Old Testament times. It disconcerts older people and infuriates people like me. Is this robotic approach down to the technology, or is the technology simply a vehicle for a deeper malaise that has spread through society?

As well as depersonalizing technology, we have seen major shifts in thinking that have resulted in a society whose enshrined values are all opposed to God, particularly when it comes to valuing older people. Speaking on BBC's *Thought for the Day*, James Jones, the Bishop of Liverpool, said:

We do not esteem the elderly for the length of years and their wisdom. Rather, we sell ourselves creams and surgery to banish all signs of aging from our own bodies. This enslavement to youthfulness would be comical if it weren't for the seriousness of what faces our aging population. Special homes for the elderly are closing under the weight of regulation. No wonder no one wants to grow old. Few politicians seem to have grasped the gravity. There is little provision or support for the extended family. There is little incentive for the young to care for the old and to uphold the commandment to honour your father and mother. Jesus reserved some of His most withering comments for those who abandoned their parents, even those claiming a religious motivation. He accused them of making void the Word of God.

Almost a year later, on the same programme, the Reverend Roy Jenkins of Cardiff made the point that the strong in society had a duty to protect the weak, 'It is not right for the strong to expect the weak to move over,' he said, but he was gone in a moment and I wondered how many people had heard what he said. Certainly not the doctors who took part in a study led by Professor Ann Bowling, of the Department of Psychology at University College London and published in *Quality and Safety in Health Care*, a specialist publication from the *British Medical Journal*. The study found that doctors in Britain regularly discriminate against older patients by denying them tests and treatments they offer to younger people. Professor Bowling commented, 'Resources are limited and doctors have to make difficult decisions. Maybe they have run out of options and are using age as an excuse.

The doctors were quite ready to justify their reasons. They may see older people as less deserving.'[1] So older people, who have paid into the NHS all their lives, must move over for the younger.

In March 2006, a report issued[2] by a coalition of three state bodies – the Healthcare Commission, the Audit Commission and the Commission for Social Care – said that poor treatment of many older people in NHS hospitals was probably because of 'deep-rooted cultural attitudes to ageing'. Several reforms were suggested, but rather than diminishing, reports of older people being poorly treated and 'swept aside' are increasing. In February 2007, an 83-year-old woman died alone after being sent home from a hospital in the Midlands in the early hours of the morning. Although records showed she lived alone, she was discharged at 4 a.m., without anyone telephoning her next of kin, despite her having dementia. No record of any treatment she received was made; all that was recorded was that she had received a cup of tea. She was discharged still wearing the orange sticky pads from an echo cardiogram, the details of which were never recorded. She was found dead in her bedroom at 2 p.m. the same day, clutching her Bible.

A week later, police in another county were probing claims of criminal negligence over the death of a once sprightly grandmother, whose daughter, a senior nurse in a GP's practice, reported seeing bandages not changed for days and ulcerated wounds infected with maggots. A hospital post-mortem said her mother had died of 'old age', but a Home Office pathologist revealed she had died from blood poisoning.

Her daughter said, 'I sat there for six weeks, and the care I saw was disgusting. No matter how much I intervened, nobody took any notice or wanted to do anything.'

These events made the headlines, but they are not isolated. A nurse at a major teaching hospital in the south made an undercover film showing how elderly patients were being treated. When broadcast on television there was outrage and promises of change for the better but, instead of being commended for her concern, the nurse was subjected to censure for breaching confidentiality, and at the last count was still suspended from duty.

This attitude to older people does not seem to be the same in other countries. Whenever I've stayed in America I've been struck by the affection shown to older people. Grandparents are particularly beloved and seem to have a next-to-God status. There is even a country music song with a refrain about there being 'holes in the floor of heaven and Grandma's watching over me'!

The physical effects of loneliness

A leading politician has described our society as 'broken', and the signs are that the number of people feeling isolated and lonely will increase. Older people appear to be particularly at risk. Researchers at Rush University's Alzheimer's Disease Center in Chicago have found a link between feelings of loneliness and developing dementia, including Alzheimer's,[3] in elderly people. The people studied were given a loneliness quiz rated on a scale from low, at one, to five for high, and tested annually for signs of memory loss and confusion, two key signs of dementia and Alzheimer's. During the study period, seventy-six individuals developed dementia that met the criteria of Alzheimer's disease. The risk of developing Alzheimer's rose by about 51 per cent for each extra point scored on the loneliness scale. A person with a loneliness rating of 3.2 had twice the Alzheimer's risk of someone with a low score of 1.4. The findings were not significantly affected by markers of social isolation, such as having a small network of friends, relatives and acquaintances, and lack of social activity, meaning that people who have a small number of good friends might be better off than those with a busy social schedule but with chronic feelings of loneliness.

'Humans are very social creatures,' said team leaders Dr Brian Wilson and Dr David Bennett. 'People who have this feeling of being socially isolated are at higher risk of developing Alzheimer's. We need healthy interactions with others to maintain our health. The results of our study suggest that people who are persistently lonely may be more vulnerable to the deleterious effects of age-related neuropathology.'

It was not the onset of Alzheimer's that caused people to feel lonely, because their loneliness levels remained relatively stable even in people who developed dementia.

Other studies show that genes with links to the immune system and inflammation in the body were more active in people who said they were lonely. More work is needed to investigate how negative emotions affect the brain, said Dr Wilson.

If loneliness is causing changes in the brain, it is quite possible that medications or changes in behaviour could lessen the effects of these negative emotions and reduce the risk of Alzheimer's disease. Several previous studies have found a link between social isolation, mental decline, and a higher risk of dementia. People who tend to be depressed and to feel overwhelmed with stress are also at greater risk for Alzheimer's. Social isolation is often brought on by being single, participating in few activities with others, or having few people in your social network.

But you can have a large network and still feel isolated. Some people report themselves as feeling socially isolated and disconnected from others even when they are surrounded by family and friends.

Strengthening connections in church

'Isolated and disconnected, even when surrounded by others in church' describes how many older people feel today. They have been filtered out of the mainstream of church life, swept aside by energies focused on youth work and evangelism. Typical of their dismay was a letter in *Joy* magazine, the journal for the British Assemblies of God. Under the subheading 'Invisible Generation', it was a plea from an older church member. 'We don't mind the new tunes, or all the youth activities,' the correspondent wrote, 'but out went the old Redemption Hymn book and why was that? We're looking for a new pastor and one who applied was turned down because he was fifty.' He hoped that the church would remember the older ones who had built it up.

In an article in *Pilgrim Homes' Quarterly Magazine*, Roger wrote about an older lady who loved to participate in Bible studies and home groups. But it became clear people thought she was too forceful, and she quoted too many scriptures to back up her points! As one of the young people put it to her, 'Jane, it's all right for you to be so certain and so forceful; you grew up in a different world. We live in an age with no certainties. We have to relate to people who have no knowledge of the Bible, and nothing is absolute you know!' But God was, and His Word was, so why couldn't they accept what she said? She knew the world was different, but there were so many things they talked about that she had been through as well, and she knew she could help them. But they didn't want the help of an old lady, and she stopped going to the home group.

I knew a 96-year-old lady, who had been a well-known Bible teacher and a strong member of her church. She began to have trouble with her legs, and felt 'tottery' and insecure. Over a period of eighteen months, she found herself out of sight and out of mind, with no one coming to visit her from her church or take her there on Sunday. I happened to speak to her vicar, who said they had assumed she was going somewhere else, but no one had thought to telephone her to check. Another example is a retired pastor whose congregation more than doubled under his leadership. Now in his eighties, he is not visited or telephoned by anyone from his former church. It would make so much difference to him to have someone take his disabled wife shopping.

'I can get the groceries,' he said, 'but she would like to have another lady shopping with her at times.'

In our homes, there are older folk who are never visited by members of their churches. It grieves our carers, because older people's memories are precious to them, especially of their church lives.

Thankfully, it is not true of all churches. The pastor of Whitby Evangelical Church told me, 'I am very aware in my own congregation of the great worth of older members. They provide the backbone of our church and many of our ministries and activities would not function without them.'

People in churches like this notice when older brothers

and sisters in Christ are having problems, and will help to arrange lifts to church, and home visits. My church is one of the few I have come across that has a slot on the front page of its notice sheet asking who needs a lift to church, and giving a telephone number to call. And churches in the countryside are more often than not still at the centre of their rural community.

Empathy, not sympathy

An old saying is that we should not judge another person until we have walked in his shoes. Shared experience is helpful in empathizing with older people, but we can't truly help elderly Christians unless we are comfortable with our own aging, and mortality. Pilgrims journeying together have the same end in sight, and, as Bunyan's *The Pilgrim's Progress* so beautifully illustrated, we are here to encourage each other.

I often wonder if the reason that under-fifties are largely unconcerned about the elderly is that they have not recognized their own mortality. Perhaps experience counts here, too; we can all identify and empathize with babies, children, teenagers and adults because we've been there, and done that. But most under-fifties have no idea of what it is like to be old. I read of someone who once went around for a whole day with an elastic band just below his knee so he could feel what it was like to have a dodgy, arthritic knee. At the end of the day he knew just what that felt like! But he still could not fully appreciate what it is really like to be old.

Yet if we looked beyond the outward appearance, beyond the stoop and the wrinkles, to the person within, we would realize how much they are like us. Think about it – do you feel different inside, now, to how you felt when you were, say, twenty-five, or thirty-five? Aren't you, at your core, still the same kid that scissor-jumped fences because it was too boring to go through the gate? Only your wearing-out body stops you doing it now, and perhaps an adult sense of decorum.

When I meet older people in our homes I find myself looking for the person beyond the frail frame in front of me, seeking their essence, the real them. Interviewing Ron, a 102-year-old, and looking beyond his missing teeth (which he refuses to wear) and his crumpled trousers (which he doesn't like changing), I found a zesty, adventurous, independent man, someone who had scrimped and scraped to buy a boat ticket to follow his sweetheart to Canada in the 1920s, and who, with no construction experience, built the family home.

I often wish I could invent a kind of breastplate for our elderly residents that would light up with a small video of them when they were in their prime, so visitors could see them as they really are.

Serita Washington put it well during a seminar we were taking at a conference one day. Serita is the wife of a pastor, a trained nurse and a specialist in caring for the elderly with dementia. She said, 'When you see Winifred tottering along the corridor on her walking frame, don't say, "The poor dear." Don't think, "Poor old thing." No – she is Winifred, the nurse at the mission who helped birth hundreds of babies.' The silent lady who has forgotten how to eat and is now being fed by a carer is Jill, a pioneering health care worker in Nepal, who fostered dozens of children and helped thousands to spiritual birth. I heard that one of the churches she founded there has 2,000 members. Her family showed me a photograph of one of her foster children, who is now a pastor.

One of our residents, suffering from depression, felt she was not worth anything. Her carers put up a life board showing the valuable work she did as a nurse and a missionary. When visiting medical professionals come, the staff proudly point out the board and the visitors look at their patient with fresh eyes and esteem.

Singer Sir Cliff Richard asked the same of the carers who looked after his mother, who was suffering with dementia. He was interviewed on television about how his family was coping. 'We want her carers to see Dorothy,' he said, 'to know how she used to be. So we've taken a photograph of her when she was well, in the prime of life, and we've hung it on the wall, near her bed. She was always full of life, friendly and interested in people.'

The deepest connection

When we committed our lives to Christ, He formed in us a connection that can never be broken. He gave us His Holy Spirit and has promised that He will never leave us. Our older folk have a good deal of life experience, and have been 'through the deep waters', and one of the joys of talking with them is hearing how God had made himself felt in all their circumstances, large and small.

After praying for guidance on a particularly difficult matter, an 84-year-old told me, 'I was washing the dishes and suddenly I knew the Lord had heard my prayer. I knew that the answer would come soon.'

One of our home managers remembers the night Beryl, a resident with dementia, could not be settled into bed. She got up and wandered around and was gently persuaded back seven times. Then the manager suggested that her friend,

Jane, should come and pray with her before she went to sleep. Beryl happily agreed, and Jane sat alongside her and prayed. Then Beryl prayed, and her friend's eyes opened wide in wonderment. She told the manager, 'Those things she prayed for I haven't mentioned to a soul, only to the Lord. It must be the Holy Spirit!' The evidence of the Holy Spirit at work happens so often in our homes that a whole book could be written about this, alone.

Often the worse the circumstances, the closer God becomes. Romanian Pastor Richard Wurmbrand, author of *Tortured for Christ*, was kept in solitary confinement in a dark, underground dungeon by the Communist regime. All human contact and all sensory input were kept to an intensely bare minimum, and the guards even wore rags over their shoes to deaden any sound. He was in the dungeon cell for three years, and imprisoned for a total of twelve. When he was released, other passengers on the bus paid his fare, knowing the horrors of the Communist system. Suddenly, he was overcome with the fear that Christ would not be as real to him outside as He had been in his cell, and he got off the bus and ran into a little copse, throwing himself to his knees. 'If You are not going to be with me here like You were in there, send me back!' he cried.

Apart from a miracle, people suffering with dementia will not experience the same release as Richard Wurmbrand, but the Scriptures promise us that they will know the closeness of the Lord and they will find 'treasure in the darkness'. The same Holy Spirit who raised Christ from the dead dwells in us. Older people with dementia have not been forsaken and they are not going through their imprisoning disease alone.

We may never know, in our lifetimes, whether the causes of dementia lie in our genes, the food we eat, our lifestyles or our social well-being, or a combination of them all. But we can be sensible about the choices we make. If loneliness predisposes to dementia, or indicates underlying needs that we, in our church families, can help alleviate, then doesn't it make sense that we should, as the Scripture says, 'Do unto others…' in the light of Matthew 25:40? It wouldn't take a lot of effort or reorganizing, because all the talents and compassion are already there. We do need to think about it. In chapters 9 and 13 we look at some ideas for helping our older brothers and sisters in Christ – and ultimately, perhaps, ourselves, too.

CHAPTER 5

The 'Ifs' that are Not Dementia

'God is our refuge and strength,
an ever-present help in trouble.
Therefore we will not fear,
though the earth give way
and the mountains fall into
the heart of the sea.'
(Psalm 46:1–2)

You can hardly visit any of the southern states of America without hearing of Jeff Foxworthy. He has published a series of witty books and CDs called *You might be a redneck if...* Redneck is a term used for people living in rural, poor communities, sometimes as a pejorative by outsiders, and with a sense of pride by rednecks themselves. Foxworthy himself comes from Atlanta, and counts himself a redneck.

'Redneck is a state of mind,' he asserts. 'There's a little of it in everyone. And Rednecks are everywhere. It's nothing to do with where you were raised.' He summed up the condition as 'a glorious absence of sophistication'. In contrast, among the over-sixties in the non-redneck population there is a good deal of sophistication, as many a young marketing manager has found to his cost. So what have Foxworthy's books got to do with dementia? It is the way he links behaviours to a defined condition. *You might be a Redneck if...* echoes the thinking of those noticing forgetful or aberrant behaviour in themselves or someone close to them. 'It could be dementia, if' – if it keeps happening, or gets worse, usually.

If 'must be the smallest word with the biggest impact in the English language. It implies a condition on which something depends and, when that condition is dementia, a good deal depends on it. You can be scatterbrained all your life and not raise eyebrows – until you reach your late fifties. Then, if you forget your keys or which day of the week it is, or put the eggs in the teapot and the tea leaves in the frying pan for breakfast you, or your family will be thinking, "It might be dementia if ..."'

In this chapter, we look at some of the 'ifs' that jump into the minds of the over-fifties. A few can be demolished fairly quickly – after all, if you were scatterbrained at sixteen, why should you be different at sixty? Your 'senior moments' were the same when you were younger, but they weren't given an age weighting. Some physical conditions can produce the same symptoms as dementia, and the good news is that most of them can be treated.

Although the *British Medical Journal*'s survey of doctors' attitudes to older people in the UK was not encouraging, nevertheless they will not dismiss an older person's symptoms as 'senility'. They will look more closely at presenting symptoms, and not automatically assume they are just a part of old age. For this, in the UK, we owe thanks to physicians like John Wedgewood, consultant geriatric physician at Bury

St Edmunds Hospital in England in the 1960s. He believed that older patients should be approached in the same way as younger patients, which meant establishing distinct diagnosis and prescriptions for each separate case. He changed the practice of geriatric medicine until it ceased to be literally a 'dead end'. In consequence, conditions previously attributed to senility were discovered to be specific illnesses which could be effectively treated.

Cardiovascular disease

One of the mysteries of aging, and a central issue that is only now being systematically addressed, is why some people age well and others do not – heading down a path that ends up in a medical condition known as frailty. Frailty involves exhaustion, weakness, weight loss and a loss of muscle mass and strength. It affects the brain as much as any part of the body, and can result in poor mental functioning. Fatigue, lapses of memory, and foggy thinking are similar to the symptoms of dementia, so it is not surprising that people begin to think, 'It could be dementia…'

Now, though, some scientists are finding that in many cases, a single factor – undetected cardiovascular disease – is a major reason people become frail. People with undetected cardiovascular disease may not have classic symptoms like a heart attack or chest pains or a stroke, but they can have partially blocked blood vessels in the brain, the legs, the kidneys or the heart. Those obstructions, in turn, can result in exhaustion or mental confusion or weakness, or a slow walking pace. It can look like incipient dementia, but it is a condition that can respond to treatment and it should be possible to delay, or even prevent, any further deterioration by treating the underlying medical condition, once it is diagnosed. It is hugely important, as the researchers at Leiden University Medical Centre showed. 'Our findings not only support the hypothesis that vascular factors contribute to dementia in the elderly, they are highly suggestive that a diminished cerebral blood flow indeed causes brain damage,' said Dr Aart Split, a Leiden radiology resident and lead author of the study.[1] 'Possible causes of low cerebral blood flow include heart failure and a narrowing of cerebral or cervical arteries.' He said that it was important to monitor both high and low blood pressure in older adults.

Anaemia

Many older people simply accept fatigue, frequent infections or lapses of attention as normal signs of aging, yet these symptoms are typical of anaemia, which happens to be a common disorder among the elderly. From the Greek meaning 'without blood', anaemia refers to a deficiency of red blood cells and haemoglobin, a protein in red blood cells. These cells are crucial for carrying oxygen from the lungs to tissues throughout the body – including the brain. If someone is anaemic, their blood is less able to transfer oxygen to their tissues and, since all human cells depend on oxygen for survival, varying degrees of anaemia can have a wide range of clinical consequences.

Janet is a trained nurse who moved across country to keep an eye on her 84-year-old, very independently minded mother. 'It would be easier if she lived with us,' she once sighed, 'but it's important for her to have her independence.' They were both concerned when her mother, a very organized lady, started losing things and forgetting appointments. Janet persuaded her to have a blood test, and she was found to be anaemic. After several weeks of medication, she was back to her old self.

A study by researchers at John Hopkins University found that among elderly women, even mild anaemia had an impact.

Senior citizens finding it difficult to think clearly may jump to the conclusion that they are experiencing the early signs of dementia. Our work supports the notion that mild anaemia may be an independent risk factor for so-called executive-function impairment in older adults

said Dr Paulo Chaves, an assistant professor at the John Hopkins University School of Medicine and the lead author of the study.[2]

If further studies confirm that's true, this could mean that correction of anaemia in these patients might offer a chance to prevent such a cognitive decline. Executive function impairment, which happens often before memory loss occurs, may occur early on in the process of becoming unable to carry on with instrumental, day-to-day living activities, such as shopping, cooking, taking medications, paying bills, walking, etc.

In other words, anaemia sneaks up on you and, like the frog in the water gradually brought to the boil, it will get you unless you recognize the danger. The good news is that it is eminently treatable. A doctor will prescribe an iron tablet, and a balanced diet. Iron is found in meat, liver, cereals, raw green vegetables, and fortified foods such as some breakfast cereals. It's a good idea to eat foods containing vitamin C at the same time as eating non-meat sources of iron because this helps with iron absorption. Good sources of vitamin C include peppers, Brussels sprouts, sweet potatoes, carrots and oranges. Instead of just cereal for breakfast, add fruit. Instead of a cup of tea or coffee with biscuits, have carrots instead.

A poor diet

Diet is important. Jeffrey Blumberg, Professor of Nutrition at Tufts University, says that many of the signs of growing older that used to be attributed to aging are actually due to a poor diet. Taking the trouble to shop for and cook nutritious food is not something that every older person can be bothered to do, especially if they are living alone. Difficulty with chewing, digestive disorders, or persistent physical and psychological problems such as arthritis, loneliness and depression are contributory factors. (There it is again: loneliness.) Older people are also susceptible to dehydration: they sense thirst more slowly and less intensely than younger people do, so those who are otherwise well may not drink enough fluids. Also, weak bladders are quite common among the elderly, and some will restrict their fluid intake because they do not want to make frequent trips to the lavatory, especially if moving is difficult. The elderly have a higher percentage of body fat and, because fat tissue contains less water than lean tissue, the total amount of water in the body tends to decrease with age. Britain's NHS Direct website (www.nhsdirect.nhs.uk/) warns, 'Even though your body is mainly made up of water, the amount of water in your body only has to decrease by a few per cent, for dehydration to occur.' It is a good idea to put bottles of water or juices (that you know they like) in the fridge for older people, and to check that they are drinking enough.

In the prolonged heatwave in France in the very hot summer of 2003 over 3,000 elderly people died, prompting comments in the press that the real scandal was that families, heading for the hills for their holidays, left their grandparents home alone. To be fair to the families, many older people prefer to stay in familiar surroundings and don't like the disruption of a holiday, and no one could have foreseen that the temperature would soar to more than 40°C and stay there for so long. But the picture that emerged is of hundreds and hundreds of 'home-alone' old folk with no one checking to see how much fluid they were drinking.

Poor absorption of vitamins

As our bodies age, they become less efficient at absorbing some essential nutrients and vitamins. Vitamin B12 is one of them. Low levels of Vitamin B12 are associated with raised levels of an amino acid called homocysteine, and that in turn is related to a higher risk of coronary heart disease, stroke and peripheral vascular disease, which in turn are linked to a higher risk of cognitive decline and dementia. In 2006, researchers from the Jean Mayer USDA Human Nutrition Research Center on Ageing at Tufts University recruited more than three hundred and twenty healthy older men from a Veterans Affairs study on aging. At baseline, all the men completed food-frequency questionnaires, and blood was drawn from each subject to measure B vitamins and homocysteine. Over the following three years, the men took occasional tests to monitor cognitive function. At the conclusion of the study, researchers reported that high homocysteine levels were associated with a decline in recall memory, while high folate levels were significantly linked to verbal fluency. Writing in the *American Journal of Clinical Nutrition*, the USDA authors concluded that 'Low B vitamin and high homocysteine concentrations predict cognitive decline.' Meat, dairy products and eggs are sources of vitamin B12.

Anti-cholesterol drugs

Statins, drugs taken to reduce 'bad' cholesterol, LDL, seem to be a mixed blessing. American scientists examined the brain tissue of 110 people who had donated their brains to research upon their death. They found there were significantly fewer of the plaques and tangles of Alzheimer's in the brains of people who had taken statins compared with those who had not. It was not a randomized controlled trial, however, and the lead author of the report,[3] Dr Gail (Ge) Li, said that people with Alzheimer's are a diverse group and 'Statins are probably more likely to help prevent the disease in certain kinds of people than others.'

Thousands of people take statins with reportedly good, cholesterol-reducing effects, but in seeming contrast to Dr Li's reports, cases where people taking statins have developed dementia-like symptoms have been reported in the States.[4] In 2001, researchers at the Max Planck Center for Molecular Medicine in Berlin discovered that cholesterol is integral to the proper functioning of synapses, the contact points between neurons responsible for, among other things, memory and learning. 'These lipids (cholesterol molecules) are like small islands or platforms on the surface of the cell,' said James Zheng, a neurobiologist at the University of Medicine and Dentistry, New Jersey. 'Embedded in these lipids are proteins that receive the brain's signals. Without the platform, the proteins become dispersed.' While statins were developed to limit the production of cholesterol in the liver, some pass easily through the blood-brain barrier, penetrating the thin membrane that encases the brain. Some scientists now believe statins, by depleting the amount of cholesterol in the brain, might be dramatically affecting neuronal communication. Neurobiologist and physician Beatrice Golomb[5] launched a Statin Study Group at the University of California-San Diego (UCSD) nearly a decade ago. It was one of the largest independent clinical trials to examine statins and cognition; a randomized controlled trial of 1,000 San Diego residents where researchers examined the effects of statins on thinking, mood, behaviour and quality of life. Preliminary analysis of the research, conducted by scientists at UCSD suggests statins can cause cognitive problems, including amnesia, forgetfulness and disorientation. The results of the trial were due to be announced at a meeting of the American Medical Association in November 2007.[6]

Other underlying causes of symptoms that can appear to be dementia are an under-active thyroid, some prescription drugs and chronic alcoholism. The first two are treatable, and so is the third, once it has been acknowledged. Alcoholism could have a big impact on the incidence of dementia in some parts of the world. In New Zealand, because of the heavy consumption of alcohol among the 'baby boomer' generation, experts are predicting increasing pressure on dementia units as they become the country's next wave of aged. Dr Nadim Khan presented a research paper at a dieticians' conference in Christchurch early in September 2007,[7] revealing that one in every twenty residents in rest homes he surveyed in Christchurch had a problem with drinking. He then took his study into the community and found an estimated one out of ten people over the age of sixty-five had a 'hazardous pattern of alcohol consumption'. The problem becoming more apparent was the increasing number of cases of alcohol-related dementia. Heavy drinking has never been the best way to keep a sound mind.

Normal pressure hydrocephalus

Brain disorders or injury can also produce symptoms like dementia. People with a little-known condition called normal pressure hydrocephalus (NPH) have been diagnosed with Alzheimer's, but when NPH was discovered and treated they returned to their former selves, much to their great joy. NPH is caused by excess fluid putting pressure on the brain. The result can be problems with gait, walking, with thinking and with bladder control – all symptoms also found with dementia. The treatment for NPH is a 45-minute procedure in which neurosurgeons surgically insert a tube called a shunt into the brain. The tube drains the excess fluid from the brain and moves it to the belly where it can be absorbed. A patient who had written his own obituary after being diagnosed with Alzheimer's some years before the correct diagnosis of NPH was so overwhelmed with his return to normality that he became a man with a mission to spread the word about NPH. He starred in a public-service announcement (a kind of advertorial, on public service TV in America) re-enacting what his symptoms were like before, and showing how he is now. Following the broadcasts,

Dr Gail Rosseau, a neurosurgeon at the Chicago Institute of Neurosurgery, received hundreds of calls from patients who had seen them, telling her, 'That sounds like me. It sounds like my mother, my father, someone that I know.' She told *CBS News* 'Patients and their families should know that if someone is aging and their gait is worsening, their mental thought processes are becoming less clear, and they have urinary incontinence, they need a scan. They need to insist on a scan and they need to see a specialist who knows about normal-pressure hydrocephalus.'

The patient, Bob Fowler, says he feels he's been given a second chance, and he wants to share it with others. 'I can spot 'em quickly,' he said. 'I've even walked up to people and had the audacity to say – have you had an MRI or a CT scan in the last few years?' He tells them he knows their gait and their walk; then urges them: 'Do yourself a favour – have a CT scan or an MRI.' CAT scans and MRIs cost money, though; an increasing consideration in the UK and America.

Depression – the worst of all

But the worst condition of all, that not only mimics dementia but can cause it, is depression. The 'worst of all' tag was given to this condition by over two hundred and fifty thousand people in sixty different countries when asked to rank the impact of long-term diseases on their health. In the largest study of its type, conducted by the World Health Organization, depression emerged as the most damaging, and the most widespread. The report, published widely in September 2007, could have added, 'particularly for the elderly', as it coincided with the publication of another study showing that in the UK the over-65s have the highest suicide rate of any age group. While 3.5 million over-65s experience mental health problems, most of those with depression or dementia are not even diagnosed, largely because of age discrimination. June Crown, chairman of the four-year UK Inquiry into Mental Health and Well-Being in Later Life, said:

> By 2021, one in 15 Britons will be an older person suffering a mental health problem, but age discrimination remains the fundamental problem ... the majority of older people with mental health problems do not receive services. Mental health problems in later life are not an inevitable part of ageing. They are often preventable and treatable, and action to improve the lives of older people who experience mental health difficulties is long overdue.

It is important that depression is treated, because it can reduce the blood flow to the brain,[8] according to research published by Professor Bonne. 'Currently, clinical psychiatry is based almost solely on subjective observer-based judgment,' said Bonne. 'Our findings suggest that objective imaging evaluations could support subjective clinical decisions.' Because the symptoms of depression and dementia are often so similar, an older person with dementia may sometimes be wrongly thought to have depression, and vice versa. (Of course, knowing that you have been diagnosed with dementia, whether Alzheimer's or not, can be a cause for depression in itself.) The main difference between dementia and depression is that, although they can be affected by the depression, a depressed person's powers of reasoning and ability to orientate themselves as to time and space usually remain intact, while in a person with dementia, they are likely to be impaired. A depressed person will usually complain of an inability to remember things but will remember when prompted, whereas a person with dementia will be forgetful but often try to cover up memory lapses.

Depression is not good for you at any age, but if you are older it can be downright deadly. Sadly, for some people, simply getting older seems to be a recipe for depression. Sometimes older people lose their self-esteem as they find they are not able to do what they once did. Old age is a time of loss, too, of physical and mental strength, of friends and family outlived and, most poignantly for Christians, of fellowship and contact with other believers. It can be a shock, too, to realize that there are more years behind you than there are in front. Until, that is, you lift your mind from the present and ponder all that is ahead.

A pastor who spoke at one of our Annual General Meetings said he saw his copy of the *Saga* magazine not as a reminder that he was growing old, but as a prompt to look beyond 'old' to putting off the mortal body and beyond that to a resurrection body and a new heaven and a new earth. The Scriptures tell us that we will gaze at Jesus with inexpressible joy. Think of worshipping with the angels! I often think, too, of the company we will enjoy. All our special, precious people will be there, and in between singing praises, I'm looking forward to conversations with David, Ruth, Deborah, Jonathan, John, Mary, Peter, Dorcas, Lazarus and so many more. The best is yet to come.

Grow old along with me!
The best is yet to be,
The last of life, for which the first was made:

> Our times are in His hand
> Who saith 'A whole I planned,
> Youth shows but half; trust God: see all, nor be afraid!
>   Robert Browning (1812–89)

In summary, some conditions that can cause symptoms that seem like dementia are:

- undetected cardiovascular disease
- anaemia
- a poor diet – and a vitamin deficiency
- not drinking enough fluids
- under-active thyroid
- some prescription drugs
- chronic alcoholism
- anti-cholesterol drugs
- other brain conditions, including normal pressure hydro-cephalus
- depression.

This is not a comprehensive list, and you should always check all symptoms with your doctor.

CHAPTER 6

Prevention

'Therefore, strengthen your feeble arms and weak knees!
"Make level paths for your feet," so that the lame may not
be disabled, but rather healed.'
(Hebrews 12:12–13)

The apostle Paul likened life to a race (1 Corinthians 9:24). Most of us would like to finish it well, to break the tape running. We know that our days are determined (Job 14:5) but we want to make the most of them, and there are forestloads of publications bursting with advice to help us. They tell us what we should eat, how to exercise our bodies and our brains, and how to guard the health of our hearts, both physically and psychologically.

Interestingly, the latter is being seen as increasingly important, which will come as no surprise to Bible-reading believers, as the Scriptures place more emphasis on the well-being of our internal landscape than the outer. 'Search me, O God, and know my heart; test me and know my anxious thoughts,' wrote the psalmist (Psalm 139:23). Proverbs 4:23 says 'Above all else, guard your heart, for it is the wellspring of life.' Increasingly, medical attention is being paid to the effects of negative emotions such depression, anger and fear, which are known to have physical reactions that affect our minds and bodies.

The Bible is full of sound instruction. '"Make level paths for your feet," so that the lame may not be disabled, but rather healed' (Hebrews 12:13) is a sensible thing to do in any number of contexts. If you know that your family is prone to certain conditions you can take steps to avoid, or at least ameliorate them. It was one of the reasons a husband and wife bought an apartment in our new extra care housing (or assisted living) complex while they were in their early sixties and in good health. The move meant relocating a few hundred miles from a different part of the country, so they were careful to weigh up the pros and cons. The husband told me, 'We believe it added an extra twenty years to my father's life, when he moved into a more relaxed environment. He lived to be eighty-seven, which was rather exceptional for his family; they had an inherited heart condition and most men in his family died from that.'

Is it possible to prevent dementia? Yes and no. From the literature it seems that until all the causes are thoroughly understood, the best we can do is keep our bodies and brains in optimum condition, doing what is good for us and avoiding what is bad. Perhaps one of our priorities should be to build brain capacity, for there are people living with dementia who, whilst they have lost some of their original capacity, had so much to begin with that, for a long while, they are able to enjoy as full a life as any of us.

An example is Christine Bryden, diagnosed in 1995 with Alzheimer's disease at the age of forty-six, then re-diagnosed with frontotemporal dementia in 1998.[1] Christine has an MBA, a Graduate Diploma in Counselling (which she obtained after being diagnosed with dementia) and a

BSc (Hons) degree in biochemistry. She was a senior executive in the Australian Prime Minister's Department, heading up the science and technology division, and was awarded the Public Service Medal in 1994. In *Dancing with Dementia* she wrote:

> My functioning seems almost normal because of my anti-dementia drugs, without which I could not travel, talk or even shower or dress. But not only have these helped, but so has my previous level of education and ability. The neurologist says it is like I used to juggle maybe as many as six balls, whereas ordinary people might juggle three at most. I might have dropped three balls now at this stage in my decline, but I still juggle almost as many balls as the ordinary person I meet each day.[2]

This reserve capacity was observed in a longitudinal study at Rush Alzheimer's Disease Center,[3] which showed that although one-third of the participants had shown no sign of cognitive decline over several years of follow-up, examination of their brains after death showed that about half of them had significant Alzheimer's disease and nearly a quarter had cerebral vascular disease. It seemed likely that these individuals had escaped the loss of memory despite the mounting damage.

Advice from the experts

Tom Kirkwood, Professor of Medicine and Head of Gerontology at the Institute for Ageing and Health at the University of Newcastle, in an interview about aging on the Open University website,[4] said:

We can make choices in life that will give our bodies the best chance of coping with the damage that attacks us. We know, for example, that tobacco causes damage to our cells ... you can also avoid sunlight that we know damages skin. But there are much more profound things that we know can build into how we try and maintain our bodies through life. Nutrition is terribly important. We can avoid foods that damage us, such as fatty foods, and we can seek out foods that we know are good for us. If we think about the things that we put into our bodies that ultimately will become part of our cellular structure and part of the maintenance system that we have, then we can hope to achieve quite a lot.

We should also think in terms of exercise. It's good for the cardiovascular system, it's good for the general well-being of the muscles and skeleton, but actually there's good evidence that exercise can play a part in slowing down the rates of certain kinds of damage that may contribute to aging.

We also see that mental exercise that tests our cognitive performance, things like crossword puzzles, learning a new language, provide a mental stimulus.

Things that engage us psychologically are also beneficial, because psychological well-being is important for physical well-being too. It's a way of maintaining our stress hormones in appropriate balance; a way of keeping us better protected against depression, a very common problem that afflicts far too many older people. So there's a lot that we can do. We have to take responsibility for our bodies. We only get one body in life; we might as well look after it if we want it to reach old age in good shape.

Researchers at the Albert Einstein College of Medicine in New York City found that something as simple as spending ten minutes talking with another person can improve memory and performance on tests. They found that people who talked to others more often – to neighbours, relatives and friends, even over the telephone – fared better on a short test of mental function. It held true for all age groups.

Protect your memory and brain

Experts from all points of the globe have issued advice on how to keep healthy as we age, and possibly help ward off diseases such as Alzheimer's. Interestingly, although the advice varies from not cooking with aluminium pots and pans to staying socially connected, the basic message is very similar to that for cardio-vascular and general health. A summary is given below:

One: Watch your blood pressure. Untreated high blood pressure over a long time reduces blood flow to the brain and other organs. This in turn means a reduction in nutrient supply, which could make the brain more susceptible to Alzheimer's. Several studies have shown that high blood pressure in mid-life means poor brain function later in life.

Two: Have your levels of cholesterol checked. There are two sorts of cholesterol: HDL and LDL. A too high level of LDL is said to lead to heart disease and to cognitive problems, and possibly to Alzheimer's. So take action to reduce LDL cholesterol, including lifestyle changes involving exercise, diet, and – if all else fails – medication.

Three: Check your B12 and homocysteine levels. Low levels of certain vitamins, including B12 and folate, lead to a high homocysteine level, which in turn is associated with Alzheimer's.

Four: Eat a diet rich in fruit and vegetables and a little wine. You probably already know that a diet rich in fruits, vegetables, whole grains and dairy produces reduces heart disease. The typical diet in the developed world is said to be high in fats and is linked to high blood pressure and mini strokes, which contribute to reduced cognitive function. There is also evidence that drinking a small amount of wine a day reduces the risk of developing dementia, though the reason for this beneficial effect does not seem to be fully understood.

Five: Protect your brain from injury. Head trauma has been linked to Alzheimer's, so do what you can to keep your head safe. That means using seatbelts and wearing helmets when cycling, skate boarding, horse riding, etc. A friend of mine who was a sister in intensive care in Addenbrooke's hospital, Cambridge, once told me how even a small fall off a bicycle – if it means hitting your head hard on the kerb – can mean severe brain damage, if you are not wearing a helmet.

Six: Have your eyes and ears checked as you get older. If you need spectacles or hearing aids – get them! To receive, process and remember, you need to have eyes and ears in good working order. This is so obvious that it is often ignored, along with that other great body of recommendations called common sense. Not only do poor vision and hearing adversely affect memory and brain function; they can also disconnect you socially.

Seven: Exercise. Exercise seems to be one of the master keys to health and to preserving and protecting memory and brainpower. Sometimes exercise is just about keeping moving. Immobility leads to all kinds of problems, including obesity. We become efficient at streamlining our lives, which can make us very lazy. Even a moderate amount of physical exercise can increase brain volume in older adults, according to a study at the University of Illinois at Urbana Champaign.[5]

Eight: Your brain – use it or lose it. Just as disuse of muscles leads to their atrophy, so does disuse of memory and brainpower.

Nine: Socialise. Throughout this book are references to the importance of having good connections with others. We are designed to work best when in relationship with others. Studies at Rush University (Chapter 3) and elsewhere underline the importance of not being isolated.

Ten: Beware of depression and stress. Both cause memory loss. We have to learn to handle stress and treat depression. *Stress: The Challenge to Christian Caring*, by Dr Gaius Davies, published by Kingsway, is an excellent book on how Christians can handle stress.

Eleven: Sleep. Some experts are now saying that getting enough sleep will one day be recognised as being as important as exercise and a healthy diet.

Eat well

Topping the tips for a healthy diet are vegetables – and fish. High levels of the fatty acid DHA found in fish could protect against dementia and Alzheimer's disease, said a study in the 'Archives of Neurology' last September.[6] The study involved nearly one thousand men and women with an average age of seventy-six years. Over nine years, ninety-nine developed dementia, including seventy-one diagnosed with Alzheimer's. Those with the highest DHA levels had a 47 per cent lower risk of developing Alzheimer's than the others. People with the highest levels ate an average of three servings of fish a week. Oily fish, such as salmon and herrings, are best.

Dr Qi Dai of Vanderbilt University and colleagues found that those who drank fruit or vegetable juices more than three times a week were 76 per cent less likely to develop Alzheimer's than those who consumed juice less than once a week. Their findings were published in the *American Journal of Medicine*.[7] Just *Go Green*, says physician nutrition specialist Dr Melina Jampolis, of Fit TV's *Diet Doctor*[8] (San Francisco, California). It is better to eat vegetables with a little butter, she advises, because fat helps with the absorption of fat soluble vitamins, of which Vitamin E may be particularly important for brain health. Just avoid too much saturated fat and avoid trans fats altogether, as both have been associated with almost twice the risk of Alzheimer's disease. Also, boost your vitamin B3 intake by eating foods like mushrooms, tuna, calf liver, halibut, asparagus, venison, lamb, turkey and chicken breast, prawns and peanuts.

Vegetables are definitely the thing, according to an article on cognitive decline in the 24 October 2007 issue of *Neurology*, especially green leafy vegetables. And it turns out that your mother was right – an apple a day, or rather two to three apples a day, could keep the doctor away. University of Massachusetts Lowell Professor Thomas Shea has found that eating apples and drinking apple juice may protect brain health and improve mental acuity throughout life, helping to stave off the onset of such disorders as Alzheimer's disease.[9]

Watch out for chemical preservatives in soft drinks, warns Professor Peter Piper, a professor of molecular biology and biotechnology at Sheffield University, and an expert on aging. He warns about sodium benzoate, a preservative found in some soft drinks. He said, 'these chemicals have the ability to cause severe damage to DNA in the mitochondria to the point that they totally inactivate it: they knock it out altogether. The mitochondria consumes the oxygen to give you energy and if you damage it – as happens in a number if diseased states – then the cell starts to malfunction very seriously.'[10] The importance of protecting mitochondria is reinforced by research published[11] by researchers from three separate centres.[12] The scientists say that as the power plant of cells, mitochondria perform many of the roles critical to cell function, use up to 90 per cent of the oxygen humans breathe, but are also among the first cellular components to be damaged by reactive radical oxygen species.[13] The only way to know whether soft drinks contain sodium benzoate is to read the labels on the cans or bottles.

Tea and cocoa

My mother was a wholefood fanatic long before it was fashionable. We were eating wholewheat, stoneground flour bread when most people thought it was horse food. She used herbal remedies and made elderflower and elderberry wines and put most soft drinks, apart from a select few, on a par with the works of the devil, but she always had a good word for a cup of tea. A good cup of tea has been a British virtue for as long as I can remember, though standards are declining, I'm sad to say. An Iranian friend in Cambridge once remarked that the tea at Addenbrooke's Hospital was so poor the hospital must be going down hill. 'If a British hospital can't get a cup of tea right, it says a lot about it,' he grumbled. Now research presented at a symposium[14] in America has described the health-giving benefits of the humble cup of tea. In studies, the theanine it contains, in combination with caffeine, enhanced the function of regions of the brain responsible for attention. It also promoted an alpha brain rhythm, known to induce a calmer, yet more alert state of mind.[15] But a cup of cocoa could be even better. Ian MacDonald, professor of metabolic physiology at the University of Nottingham, used magnetic resonance imaging (MRI) to detect increased activity in specific areas of the brain in individuals who had consumed a single drink of flavanol-rich cocoa. The effect is linked to dilation of cerebral blood vessels, allowing more blood – and therefore more oxygen – to reach key areas of the brain. The findings, unveiled at one of the biggest scientific conferences in America, raise the prospect of ingredients in chocolate being used to treat vascular impairment, including dementia and strokes, and thus for maintaining cardiovascular health.[16] I have always thought the cocoa bean to be one of God's kindest provisions, though I doubt the treatments will include actually eating bars of chocolate.

Exercise your brain

Schlomo Breznitz, psychology professor and former president of Israel's University of Haifa, says that scientists have known for decades that brain decay is not inevitable, because long-term studies have shown that some minds stay relatively sharp while others decline dramatically. He has developed a brain-training programme called Mind Fit which tests short-term memory and reaction time. In the UK, it was given the backing of neuroscientist Baroness Greenfield, who helped launch it at the House of Lords.

Computer console company Nintendo also produces a brain workout programme, and Professor Ryutaro Kawashima of Japan's Tokyo University said its games increase the delivery of oxygen, blood and amino acids to the brain, leading to the creation of connections between brain cells. Several companies are trying to document the effectiveness of their cognitive training products. Dakim, maker of the brain trainer [m]Power, is planning clinical trials with the University of California, Los Angeles. Posit Science, maker of Brain Fitness Program 2.0, sponsored a study published last year in the *Proceedings of the National Academy of Sciences*, showing that users improved not only in the tasks they practised, but also in unrelated memory tests – with benefits continuing three months later. It is a growing industry, with websites such as HappyNeuron.com offering mind gyms, and blogs like SharpBrains.com. This kind of software appeals not only to technophiles like me, but to hundreds of people in retirement homes in North America. It is worth investigating, because the benefits of short-term cognitive training persist for as long as five years, according to a study of older adults by the National Institute on Ageing (NIA) and the National Institute of Nursing Research (NINR).

Read Shakespeare or the Authorized Version

If you do not like technology, you can turn to language. Shakespeare is good for your brain, say researchers at the University of Liverpool. They are looking to see if wrestling with the differently structured use of language could help to prevent dementia. (Good news for aficionados of the original Authorized Version of the Bible.) Monitoring participants with brain-imaging equipment, they found that certain lines from Shakespeare and other great writers such as Chaucer and Wordsworth caused the brain to spark with electrical activity because of the unusual words or sentence structure.[17] And researchers at York University in Toronto say that people who are bilingual and speak both languages every day for most of their lives can delay the onset of dementia by up to four years, compared with those who know only one language.[18] The *Western Mail* in South Wales was quick to pounce on this story and ran it with the headline, 'Learn Welsh and fight off the onset of dementia'.

Changing routines can also spark the brain. Try putting on your shoes starting with the left foot, if you usually start with the right. We become more efficient at what we do the older we get, and our brains go into 'sleep mode', like an idling computer. Changing your routines, deliberately, moves your brain out of its 'automatic' mode and gives it a mini 'workout'.

Renew the spirit of your mind, and don't put up with depression

A growing body of evidence is showing the usefulness of cognitive behavioural therapy (CBT), for treating depression and anxiety in older people, including some with dementia.

Sometimes older people lose their sense of purpose, along with their self-esteem, as they find they are not able to do what they once did. CBT is particularly helpful for Christians because it is built on sound, scriptural principles, though secular practitioners may be surprised to hear this. But why should we be surprised? 'Every good and perfect gift is from above, coming down from the Father of the heavenly lights' said James in the New Testament (James 1:17). CBT helps bring negative thinking to light and challenges it by looking at the reality of the situation, then replacing negative thoughts with the truth. Although the National Institute for Health and Clinical Excellence recommended CBT for individuals in the early stages of Alzheimer's as long ago as 2003, access has been limited – usually shorthand for not enough resources to meet demand. CBT is one of the approaches becoming more available at local Christian counselling centres, and the Association of Christian Counsellors will be able to supply addresses (www.acc-uk.org). While research shows that CBT is effective, it may not suitable for every individual, and medication can also be very effective. Take whichever route is best for you, because depression should be investigated and treated.

Nurture your spirit

We want to be able to say with Paul that we have fought the good fight, that we have finished the race, that we have kept the faith. It makes sense that we should look after ourselves as well as we can now, but equally that we should prepare for the life that we are destined for. Thus, when I travel to the States to visit my sons, I wear British-weight clothes to the airport, but my bags are packed with clothes for California.

With its evangelical Christian basis, Pilgrim Homes has always believed that the spiritual care of elderly Christians is central to all caring, and closely linked to the individual's wholeness. For us, Matthew 25:40 is not just a text on a wall, but has always underpinned all the Society's thinking and planning.

In secular care there has been growing recognition of the importance of spirituality and its links with health and well-being. There is even a new Center for Spirituality and the Mind at the University of Pennsylvania.[19] The Center brings together some twenty experts from fields including medicine, pastoral care, religious studies, social work and bioethics. One of their studies, using imaging technology, observed the brains of Pentecostal Christians speaking in tongues, then again when they were singing gospel music. Researchers found that when the Pentecostals were speaking in tongues they showed decreased activity in the brain's language centre, compared with the singing group. Researchers said they believe that speech is taken over by another part of the brain while they are speaking in tongues, but did not find it during the study. Among other changes, both groups showed decreased activity in the parts of the brain that have to do with sense of self and spatial orientation, which suggests the description of oneness with God, of transcendence, sometimes experienced in meditation or prayer. 'For if I pray in a tongue, my spirit prays, but my mind is unfruitful,' says 1 Corinthians 14:14.

There is agreement that beliefs affect every part of our lives, and make us who we are. They are the essence of our being, but there are differing definitions of spirituality. Some say that spirituality is a search for the meaning of life. Dr Andrew Newberg, director of the centre in Pennsylvania, is one of those who hold that spirituality doesn't have to equate to religious faith. 'The feelings of enlightenment and well-being some derive from religion can come to others from artistic expression, non-religious meditation, watching a beautiful sunset or listening to stirring music.'

These are all lovely things in themselves, and these feelings are important for our well-being. But the understanding of spirituality that this book refers to is theological, based on the Bible. It means that we are not dependent on external experiences to lift us up, but on the Holy Spirit who works within us (Romans 8:9). The key difference is that the Holy Spirit is *active* in us, and a spiritual experience comes from something He does, not from our emotions. (Some relevant verses are: John 14:17; John 16:13; Galatians 4:6; 1 Corinthians 3:16; 6:19; Romans 8:1,16; 2 Timothy 1:14; Ephesians 1:17; Colossians 1:9.)

Spirituality starts either from 'below', or 'above', explains David F. Wells, Professor of Systematic and Historical Theology at Gordon-Conwell Theological Seminary, Massachusetts.

One sees saving spirituality as natural to the self. The other sees it as given to the self. One starts with human experience, the other with divine revelation. One is self-sufficient. The other understands its debt to unearned, divine grace.

Modern spirituality ... wants no doctrines, no fixed points, no public practice, and no institutions. It is, in fact, a perfect adaptation to our postmodern world. It is private, internal, individualistic, unburdened by rules, free from others, and self-focused. It is the inevitable product of our over-psychologised world.

> And the focus of this spirituality (which takes many forms) is always therapeutic.
>
> The essential difference between spirituality from above and spirituality from below is that of control. Do we control our access to God, doing it our way, or does He? How we answer this question will determine whether God becomes like us, or whether we become like Him.[20]

A beautiful sunset won't help us find the meaning of life, unless it turns our minds to seeking the One who made it. Stirring music is wonderful and, indeed, I hope to have cymbals as well as harps in heaven. But as much as I love Tchaikovsky's 1812, or Beethoven's Fifth, the music that stirs me most is that which resounds with the Spirit within me; music like the simple, yet profoundly stirring, 'Amazing Grace', written by a converted slave-trader, and 'How great Thou art!', sung by Christians in different languages all over the world.

Someone I knew once was translating some of the old Welsh hymns into English. He found it very slow going, not because of difficulties with the languages, because he was fluent in both, but because he kept getting caught up, as he put it, 'in the glory of God in the words'. As Colossians 1:27 says, it is 'Christ in you, the hope of glory.'

In summary – the experts say:

- take sensible steps in the light of your family history
- always remember that we are pilgrims, on our way Home
- have a good diet
- avoid soft drinks containing sodium benzoate

- drink tea and cocoa
- make sure your blood pressure is at a good level
- take regular exercise
- protect your brain – wear a helmet for certain sports
- have your eyesight and hearing checked
- socialize – stay connected – and talk to others often
- get depression treated
- build your brain capacity
- read Shakespeare or/and the Authorized Version of the Bible
- change your routines
- draw close to God.

CHAPTER 7

Diagnosing Dementia

'Neither height nor depth, nor anything else in all
creation, will be able to separate us from the love
of God that is in Christ Jesus our Lord.'
(Romans 8:39)

'Living with death' was the headline of a story in the *Irish Independent*.[1] It's the story of Jacinta Kennedy, who was diagnosed with Alzheimer's in 2001. She forgets things. She has trouble recalling people's names and she probably can't tell you what happened an hour ago, let alone the day before. She also has problems following a particular train of thought and, by the end of a sentence, may have already forgotten what it was she wanted to say when she began. She has a happy marriage, yet her husband Paul says that it would not be true to say that all was fine until Alzheimer's came along. In her early twenties, his wife began to suffer from depression, and he had to take over the running of the house. They are no stranger to Alzheimer's: six of Jacinta's siblings have already died from the same disease. Despite her memory problems, Jacinta is quite aware of what is going on. When asked what it means to her to travel this hard road called

Alzheimer's, she says bluntly, 'Death.' Paul confirms this: 'Yes, this is what it means to her.'

Paul says Jacinta finds it difficult to be logical and he can't leave her as she quickly gets flustered. 'Sometimes, I want to have a shower and even though the [connecting] doors are open, she will panic. She is afraid. It's like having a child in the house. I have to dress her and do everything for her. I can't leave her for even two minutes. But still I love her and always will.'

The vulnerability of people with dementia catches your heart. I was in a meeting with a group of our managers and Maureen, our Director of Housing and Care Services, when a telephone call came through from one of our sheltered housing schemes. It was late afternoon, and the housing scheme manager was due to go off duty, but thought that an occupant might need an X-ray on her ankle to see if it was broken or just badly sprained. Unusually, none of our voluntary supporters in the area could be found to take her to the hospital. (Among our supporters' strong points is accompanying and visiting individuals in hospital.) One solution was to call an ambulance, but there was the possibility that the lady might have to stay in the hospital for several hours, at least. (In Great Britain, in our National Health Service hospitals, the lines of people waiting for an X-ray move slowly at the best of times; then afterwards there's a long wait to see the consultant.) People living in sheltered housing are more independent than those in residential care, so I asked why, when the ambulance came, she couldn't go with the paramedics by herself.

'She's beginning to be a bit confused,' said Maureen.

Sympathetic eyes signalled understanding to each other, and then one of the managers said to me, 'We couldn't let her go by herself. We know she's not a child, and we don't treat her as a child, but it would feel to us like leaving a child on its own – we can't do it.'

In the event one of the staff, who should have been off-duty, came and helped out.

The headline of Jacinta's story must have caught many readers' eyes, and it certainly caught mine. 'Living with death'. How awful to see those words, emboldened in a newspaper story and, beyond that, emboldened in a life. Yet, in a very real sense it describes every person on earth. Of all the certainties of life, death is one – along with taxes, as someone once dryly commented. There are many references to death in the Bible. It is what you believe happens after physical death that determines whether or not, as poet Dylan Thomas wrote, you 'rage, rage, rage against the dying of the light',[2] or you agree with Paul, who, steeped in the Scriptures and anchored in Christ, wrote to believers at Philippi 'For to me, to live is Christ, and to die is gain' (Philippians 1:21). I have often thought how important it is for Christians to reflect a godly view of death to the world, and not absorb the world's view of it. Saying goodbye to a loved one is grievous, but less so if you know the parting is temporary.

Even so, having accepted that we are all going to die one day, we hope that it will happen quickly, painlessly and peacefully – preferably in our sleep. This is something we would like for ourselves, our family and our friends. We would not choose a lingering process that seems like the ancient Chinese 'death by a thousand cuts', nor one where the essence of us seems to slowly wizen, leaving only a shell of what we once were.

Who will ever forget the words of former American President Ronald Reagan, when he announced that he had

Alzheimer's disease? 'When the Lord calls me home, whenever that may be, I will leave the greatest love for this country of ours and eternal optimism for its future ... I now begin the journey that will lead me into the sunset of my life.' Yet the Reagans' sad journey would have started long before his announcement in 1994. There would have been lapses of memory and difficulties with language that must have seemed startlingly out of place in a man used to memorizing scripts and debating about policy.

Of all our possessions, arguably our memories are the most precious. To a large extent, our personalities are formed and reinforced by our memories. If we, or someone close to us, are having memory lapses our best hope is that it is just the normal forgetfulness that often accompanies growing older. For younger people, in their forties or fifties, memory lapses can be a sign that they are stressed, or have too much on their minds. Some of them worry that they are developing dementia. Judy McLaren, a doctor in the UK, says she once ran a test on one of her patients, just to reassure him. But people who are really developing dementia rarely present themselves, she added. Their relatives will come in with their concerns, first. Individuals themselves may be afraid of hearing the worst, or perhaps they have the 'slowly boiled frog' syndrome, and are not noticing what is happening. It is often the latter. Christine Bryden said that

> The first signs of dementia are very gradual changes in ourselves, so that we hardly notice it. Our family and friends might think we are not ourselves, and we might think we are just stressed. But it is the beginning of a long, slow journey of change. I felt foggy in my head and became more readily confused. I was

very tired, and just wanted to come home from work and sleep.[3]

It was a sense of something having changed that alerted consultant psychiatrist Dr Daphne Wallace a few years ago. Dr Wallace[4] was appointed as a consultant old-age psychiatrist in Leeds in 1979. She was involved in setting up a specific service for older people with mental health problems and fighting for resources, particularly for those with dementia. In 2004, she was under a lot of stress, and was suffering from depression. After she had recovered, she found she was still having problems; she says she knew that something had changed, even though friends told her, 'That's not dementia, we've all got that.' She sensed a loss of 'a larger capacity in certain areas', for example, in her spatial visualization and ability to navigate. She took advice from senior psychiatrists (who were also friends) and they agreed she should be referred to see a specialist. Daphne was diagnosed with very early vascular dementia in August 2005. 'It can't be cured, but it can be ameliorated,' she said. She gives talks to churches and lectures at conferences, writes literature and has been accepted by the Halle Choir. 'You should not do so much that you get stressed, but you work out what you want to do and you go on doing it,' she said.

Can't smell the roses?

If you have had a normal sense of smell all your life, but find that you can't smell the roses any more, you may have mild cognitive impairment, or a very early sign of Alzheimer's, according to Dr Robert Wilson's team at Rush Alzheimer's Disease Center.[5] 'It has been known for some time that the brain regions first affected by Alzheimer's are the olfactory centres,' Dr Wilson said. The study involved 589 community-dwelling people with an average age of eighty years. Other, better known, warning signs are

- personal hygiene deteriorating, perhaps a stain on clothing the person does not notice, or forgetting to comb their hair every morning
- increasing memory loss for day-to-day activities, such as forgetting names of people, places or objects
- just not being able to recall something, and forgetting simple words, sometimes replacing them with less appropriate words
- disruption of normal routine without being aware of it
- disorientation in time and place, becoming lost and not knowing how to get home
- not wanting to get dressed and leave the house
- sleeping more than usual
- not taking care of their home as well as they normally do
- worsening judgment, such as dressing inappropriately for the weather, or not seeking help for a serious problem
- losing abstract reasoning, such as understanding the significance of events or the ability to understand a principle
- misplacing things, even placing things in strange places, sometimes becoming paranoid or suspicious because they have disappeared
- rapid mood swings for no apparent reason
- personality change, becoming apathetic, confused, suspicious or fearful
- loss of initiative, to the point the person may not spontaneously engage in any activities.

People will usually try to ignore, or cover up, developing problems like these. Some, with good social skills, are adept at engaging others in conversation to cover up a gaffe, or divert attention away from an inadequacy. They will struggle along, with support from friends and family, as long as possible, before going to their doctor. If they have a degree of independency, they may not want others to know what is happening, though relatives will have noticed. Understandably, during this period any number of emotions can set in, including depression, anxiety, or anger.

The diagnosis

As a rule, the sooner a disease is diagnosed and treated, the better the outcome, but by the time someone has been diagnosed with Alzheimer's, the disease has typically been at work for years, and tissue damage has already occurred. Scientists believe that conditions causing dementia can begin to take hold as many as twenty years before diagnosis. The average time between symptoms becoming obvious and diagnosis is from two to three and a half years, according to a recent survey of caregivers.[6] To Greg Cole, Associate Director of Research for the Geriatric Research Education and Clinical Center at Los Angeles Veterans Medical Center, 'It's like termite damage,' he said, 'You want to repair the damage before they destroy your house.'[7]

Dr Madhav Thambisetty, part of the research team at the Institute of Psychiatry at King's College London, said, 'The frustration for so many people has been that by the time you are diagnosed with Alzheimer's, it is effectively too late to do much about it. The challenge has been to find what may cause Alzheimer's and to see if we can identify it before it sets in and therefore give patients an opportunity to have effective treatment.'[8] Dr Thambisetty and his team are working towards a blood test for dementia that could be done at local doctors' offices. The blood tests could also help show how severe the disease has become, as certain proteins are linked to changes in the brain and different stages of Alzheimer's. The test might be available within five years.

Although the health maxim holds that the earlier the diagnosis of a disease, the more effective the treatment, none of the technology mentioned by researchers, such as MRIs, PET and CT scans, seems to be routinely used as part of diagnostic procedures today. The criteria currently in use were established in 1984, and involve a two-step approach of evaluating functional disability and then looking for a cause, the result being that diagnosis and treatment are delayed until patients have significant dementia symptoms.

Dr Feldman, a senior investigator with the Brain Research Centre (BRC) at University of British Columbia Hospital[9], said, 'We now have advanced diagnostic tools – distinctive and reliable biological indicators that can be detected before the patient crosses the dementia threshold of disability.' In addition to the standard subjective observations, new guidelines he and his colleagues propose include MRIs, an examination of patients' cerebrospinal fluid, PET scans, and looking for a genetic mutation for Alzheimer's within patients' immediate families.

Very shortly, thanks to two determined Israeli scientists, it will be possible to sit behind a computer and take a simple set of neuropsychological tests, all by yourself. The lack of good, inexpensive predictive tests so vexed Dr Vered Aharonson and Professor Amos Korczyn (two leading experts) that they devoted four years of their own free time to produce a computerized evaluation test, with a difference. The NexSig computer test can be done, without an instructor, by anyone, whether or not they are used to using a computer. It measures what you do and how you do it, then analyses your performance and gives an assessment. After proving its worth in initial tests, the NexSig was launched and is already being used in some major American hospitals. Dr Aharonson says NexSig will be used extensively, as many people are worried about developing dementia as they grow older.

It may all be down to a simple blood test, if a development announced in *Nature* magazine in October 2007 proves to be effective. A Californian biotech company said it had created a diagnostic blood test that had been shown to be 90 per cent accurate. Working with colleagues in American and European universities, the test was developed by 'listening' to how 120 molecules, which function as chemical messengers between blood, brain and the immune system, communicate. There are hopes that the blood test may be able to predict the onset of symptoms of Alzheimer's up to six years ahead. It would give people time to make plans; but at present there is still no cure for Alzheimer's.

At present in the UK, the first step to diagnosis is taken in a primary care setting: that is, at the GP's surgery. Doctors use the Mini Mental State Examination (MMSE), a series of questions and tests, each of which scores points if answered correctly. If every answer is correct, there is a maximum score of thirty points. People with dementia generally score twenty-six points or less. An abbreviated Mental Test is also widely used in the UK, where one point is scored for each correct answer. You will be asked:

1. Your age
2. Time, to the nearest hour
3. Address for recall at end of test: 42 West Street (Patients are asked to repeat the address to ensure it has been heard correctly)
4. The year
5. The name of hospital, or doctor's office
6. Recognition of two persons, e.g. doctor, nurse
7. Date of birth
8. Year of start of First World War
9. Name of the Monarch
10. Count backwards from twenty to one.

A low score is followed by a referral to a memory clinic, where diagnosis is more sophisticated. A specialist consultant may arrange for a brain scan, especially if vascular dementia is suspected. The scan will show if there are any infarcts, or arterial blockages in the brain, and also if there is any other pathology, for example, a brain tumour. Individuals with Alzheimer's may well have areas of brain that are smaller, and reducing in size, but these changes can also occur in others, who have no symptoms.

Better, simpler tests

Meanwhile, researchers all over the world are looking for better, simpler ways of diagnosis. A team led by Deborah Barnes, Assistant Professor of Psychiatry at the University of California, San Francisco, is using a special 'bedside' formula to try to predict an individual's dementia risk. Based on variables such as age, cognitive function and physical performance, the index is an inexpensive, fast and practical test that groups individuals into low, medium and high-risk categories. The tool is akin to similar methods for calculating the risk of cardiovascular disease or diabetes, and predicts with up to 88 per cent accuracy whether an individual will develop dementia over the next six years. Professor Barnes says the index can provide comfort to those least likely to develop disease, while motivating those at higher risk to adopt a healthier lifestyle. It also helps families plan for the future, she says.

At Harvard Medical School researchers are working on a low-power laser to observe features of the eye.[10] They believe that scanning the eyes with lasers could help detect signs of Alzheimer's even before symptoms of the illness appear in the brain. Dr Tien Yin Wong of the University of Melbourne Centre for Eye Research also believes that examining the blood vessels in the retina of the eye for disease can help predict the risk of developing dementia. Dr Wong and his colleagues studied retinal photographs of 2,211 people aged sixty-nine to ninety-seven years. More than half had high blood pressure. In subjects with high blood pressure, retinopathy doubled the likelihood of having dementia. No such relationship was seen in those without high blood pressure.[11]

A new screening tool for dementia called SLUMS, developed by geriatric experts at St Louis University School of Medicine, is said to identify mild cognitive problems in the elderly better than the commonly used Mini Mental Status Examination. The SLUMS is currently used at many Veterans Administration hospitals, and can be downloaded free from the website.[12]

To tell, or not to tell?

In 1961, 90 per cent of doctors said they would prefer not to tell cancer patients their diagnosis. By 1977, a complete reversal of opinion had occurred, with 97 per cent of doctors favouring telling.[13] The reasons for not telling cancer patients their diagnosis in 1961 were similar to those now given for not telling patients with Alzheimer's their diagnosis. The change in policy among doctors coincided with advances in the management and treatment of cancer. Similar advances are being made with Alzheimer's disease today, so clinicians must decide whether to respect the wishes of family members not to tell patients their diagnosis, or to respect individual autonomy, inform patients, and involve them in the management of their condition.

Most relatives of patients with Alzheimer's did not want the patient to be told the diagnosis. They thought it would avoid deepening anxiety and depression. On the other hand, most of those researched said they would want to know themselves if they developed the condition. It is a complex issue. Early in 2007, a newspaper headline read, 'Professor commits suicide after catching dementia from tick bite'. The story began, 'One of the country's top experts on modern life may have killed himself after catching a rare brain disease from a tiny insect bite.' The decision to disclose the diagnosis depends very much on the individuals involved. Many patients are aware of their progressive cognitive deficits, regardless of whether or not a diagnosis of Alzheimer's has been given. Some may even be relieved that there is a reason for what is happening to them. The report in the *British Medical Journal*[14] said that family members as well as patients respond in various ways to the psychological threats presented by the diagnosis, and the issue of disclosure needs to be dealt with on a patient-by-patient basis.

Maureen, the director mentioned earlier in this chapter, who is also a trained nurse, says, 'We naturally want to protect the people we love, and wrap them in cotton wool so they don't get hurt. Some feel that their loved ones won't cope if they know the truth, but sometimes I think it is the fact that they are the ones who would have difficulty coping. While the individual doesn't know, you don't have to discuss with them the problems and the difficulties that have to be faced in the future – perhaps it is easier not having to cope with the other person's questions, fears, emotions and tears whilst trying to come to terms with your own.

'There is still the British "stiff upper lip" here; some people find it very difficult to show their emotions, to grieve together, to mourn together the probable loss of what you have had together. For some, having to confront and deal with it before it gets that bad is just too much, and it is easier to just cope when you have to. By then, though, it is often too late to share it.'

The wonderfully compassionate Dr Sacks had a similar judgment call with Dr P., the patient of the book title who actually did mistake his wife for a hat.[15] Dr P. was suffering from a brain pathology that was 'advancing towards a profound visual agnosia, in which all powers of representation and imagery, all sense of the concrete, all sense of reality, were being destroyed.' Dr P. was an unusually talented musician, and a teacher at a music school. Dr Sacks thought that music, for him, had taken the place of image. He had no body image, but he had body music; he could move and act fluently, but came to a total, confused stop if the 'inner music' stopped. And this, mercifully, held to the end – for, despite the gradual advance of his disease, Dr P. lived and taught music to the last days of his life.

Years before he died, he had asked Dr Sacks what was wrong. After examination and much thought, Dr Sacks replied, 'I can't tell you what I find wrong, but I'll say what I find right. You are a wonderful musician, and music is your life. What I would prescribe, in a case such as yours, is a life which consists entirely of music. Music has been the centre; now make it the whole, of your life.' This is imagery that speaks powerfully to the Christian soul, too; not of music, but of the presence of God.

Empathy and understanding in the Scriptures

Roger used to run the largest day unit for dementia suffers in the UK. Then his mother developed dementia, and lived until her death in one of our care homes. She was one of those people mentioned earlier who, despite confusion and absence of communication, would pray meaningfully and compassionately, and was an inspiration at the home's prayer meetings. When Roger gives seminars he talks from personal, as well as professional experience, and as a pastor, with a scriptural perspective. He says that we can understand what people with dementia are suffering from what has been written in the Scriptures.

'The slide into dementia can be frightening. At the onset sufferers won't recognize it as an illness, and will feel that they are becoming inadequate. They may try to compensate for what they see as their failings, and try to cover up the odd things they do. They will feel guilt, self-blame, and condemnation. There will be a loss of initiative, control, and confidence. They will lose that lifetime assurance of how they view themselves, the world around them, and even God. Filled with uncertainty, they can grow suspicious of people, some of whom will react by avoiding them, thus reinforcing their feelings of rejection and being misunderstood.

'There is empathy and understanding in the Scriptures. We see people struggling with the same emotions, though not the same cause. For example, Psalms 31 and 41 illustrate the process the writer is going through. He is blaming himself for the circumstances he finds himself in; is fearful and suspicious, feeling that everyone is against him. "My enemies say of me in malice, 'When will he die...?' Whenever one comes to see me he speaks falsely, while [in] his heart [he] gathers slander; then he goes out and spreads it abroad" (41:6). These verses are an expression of the emotional experience of the Lord Jesus Christ as He faces the prospect of the cross, but which also describe the turmoil and grief of people with dementia.

'Always remember Jesus' promise in John 14: "I go to prepare a place for you." They are going somewhere better, where there's no sickness or pain, no sorrow or confusion or dementia – a place where Christian pilgrims are completely at home. One day soon they're going to be walking around heaven absolutely whole, more alert and intelligent than they've ever been.'

CHAPTER 8

Listening

'In the same way, the Spirit helps us in our weakness. We
do not know what we ought to pray for,
but the Spirit Himself intercedes for us with
groans that words cannot express.'
(Romans 8:26)

The importance of listening

In all the thousands of words published about dementia,
until fairly recently, one voice has been noticeably smaller
than the others – the voice of dementia sufferers, themselves.
It is quite noticeable – in most of the literature there is still a
sense that things are being done for them and to them, but
not often with them; they are being studied, scanned,
X-rayed and 'case-studied', but not consulted. There seems to
be almost an expectation by the majority of dementia sufferers, that they are not expected to say anything, so do not
expect to be listened to. Even in dedicated internet chat
rooms, places where they can post questions and comment,
anonymously, on every topic under the sun, their exchanges
are few, and hesitant. 'It is not always easy for us to ask for
help, we do not always know the right questions…' began a
posting in an Alzheimer's chat room.

It is such a comfort to know that God is so in tune with us that He understands our thoughts, and even knows what we are going to say before we do ourselves (Psalm 139:4). He not only hears us, He *actively* listens to us, all the time. A lady with dementia, who had barely communicated in the last years of her illness, unexpectedly turned to her daughter and said, 'Remember, dear, God never forgets you.' She died a few days later.

The act of listening, of giving active attention, is one of the most important things in life for human beings, from a tiny infant to the most aged person. Most of the time we listen only half-heartedly, with part of our minds somewhere else, but if you are caring for someone with dementia you have to give them your wholehearted attention.

There is more than one arena where listening is essential for the well-being of people with dementia. First there is the public arena, inhabited by the National Health Service and lobbyists and charities, where attitudes are formed that dictate the drugs and care available. Then there is the person's own, intimate circle of family and friends; and finally there is an arena that not all dementia sufferers will enter, which includes nursing and care homes. *Listening – or not –* in each arena has a profound effect on the lives of people with dementia. Before gathering information, before making decisions, before actually doing anything, in a civilized world there has to be *listening*.

In the public arena

Listening to people with dementia could be one of the most powerful tools in the management of the disease, says Dr Kenneth Rockwood, professor of both Alzheimer's research and geriatric medicine at Dalhousie University in Canada.[1] Speaking in Australia as a guest of Alzheimer's Australia, to mark Dementia Awareness Month (September 2007), he said: 'While dementia research has made great progress in the last twenty years, there is a long way to go in having the evaluative tools that help clinicians in assessing the value of different treatments. Our latest research shows that while batteries of neuro-psychological tests assist in classifying groups of people they do not translate to whether a given treatment is helping a given individual. A person's own insight and experience may well help to improve the level of care and medical treatment that we can offer to people with dementia.

'In our study, it was the job of the skilled clinicians listening to the person with dementia and their carer to make judgments about whether particular treatments were benefiting the particular individual. While the groups who benefited clinically on average scored better on the standard tests, the match was far from exact. Many patients who did worse on the standard tests actually showed significant clinical improvement. The relevant questions are whether the person's quality of life is improved and whether the treatment is working for the individual.'

Listening to people with dementia, after asking the right questions, is the key to deciding which dementia drugs should be made available in Australia, believes Glenn Rees, the National Executive Director of Alzheimer's Australia. He said, 'There may be as many as 140 dementia drugs currently in trial. Some of these are likely to complete final trials and come to the market over the next three to five years. If the wrong questions are being asked now it can be guaranteed that there will be a long and difficult decision-making process about whether the medications are effective and should be made available under the PBS (Pharmaceutical Benefits Scheme). People with dementia want – and deserve – the assurance of early access to new medications that have been shown in trials to be safe and offering some benefits.'

In a talk given at the launch of Dementia Awareness Month in Queensland, in September 2007, he asked why, when we all want to be treated as individuals, are there such mixed reports from older people of their experiences of the nation's services? He said, 'I suggest that it is largely because we have a good system of aged care, but not one structured to empower the consumer. Arguably the predominant societal concerns are with security and dependency and institutionalization.' In other words, the focus was not on the individual needing the care.

This is how it was in 1995, when Christine Bryden was diagnosed with Alzheimer's.[2] When she tentatively rang the number of the Alzheimer's Association, the voice on the other end of the phone asked who she was caring for, her mother, or father, or husband? Christine said, 'Actually, it's me who has been diagnosed. Is there anything you have for people with dementia?' The response was that there was really very little available that would be suitable, as most material was directed towards the carer 'who was supposedly at home looking after me, in my incapacity and my inability to communicate. I put down the phone, feeling cast adrift,' she remembers.

Part of the problem may have been that Christine was diagnosed at an early age (just forty-six), and dementia is generally a disease of old age. Dementia and old age suffer the same stigma, and the sea change we are seeing today is thanks, in part, to the efforts of Christine and people like her.

She and friends in the USA and Canada, who also had a diagnosis of dementia and were able to communicate, were determined to speak out, to challenge the accepted view of the late stages of the disease.

'Most of us were taking anti-dementia drugs, and were not willing to accept being categorised into a medical model of decline according to set stages,' she wrote, 'how were we going to challenge the idea of being the "patient", or the "sufferer", and let the world know we were individuals each struggling with a terminal illness?'[3]

The vehicle they used was the Dementia Advocacy and Support Network International (DASNI),[4] which they saw as 'the beginning of a long journey to change attitudes beyond our local region'. The network is an online community with a number of websites, which aims, among other things, to make sure that people with dementia are heard, to influence decisions made on their behalf and to change people's attitudes towards them. Working via the internet, its reach is international.[5] DASNI provides a forum for exchanging information and encourages support mechanisms such as local groups, counselling groups and internet links. Approximately one-third of DASNI's members have dementia. Other members include care partners and healthcare professionals.

One DASNI website states:

The stigma of dementia is very real, very cruel and widespread. There is also a lack of knowledge about dementias, the impact of new medications, and the support available. By sharing their hopes and concerns, and participating in dementia-related activities, DASNI empowers people with dementia to actively participate in their own care and treatment. We support a more accepting, more hopeful view of living with dementia. We encourage people to improve the quality of their own life by advocating for others.[6]

Slowly and surely, the opinions of people with dementia are being taken into account. Until a few years ago, dementia care could be viewed as a sort of pyramid, with the apex inhabited by the medical experts, below them the professional carers, below them family carers and at the bottom layer, the people with dementia themselves.[7] Intellectualized and removed, decisions and options cascaded down from the people at the top to the passive sufferers at the bottom.

'People with Dementia: The Bright New Face of Global Advocacy' was the headline of an American newsletter in 2002. 'Baby boomers ... will become increasingly vocal and active in encouraging the medical, scientific, and public policy communities to listen to their needs and to welcome them as participants in their care,' said Sanford Auerbach MD, Board Chair of the Alzheimer's Association in Massachusetts. 'They will accept neither a practice of medicine seen as paternalistic, nor an image of themselves as a "burden" on society with regard to the cost or care necessitated by their illness.'[8]

Turning a deaf ear

Perhaps they should come to the UK and talk to the National Institute for Clinical Excellence (NICE), which seems to have chosen not to listen to thousands of people with dementia. NICE does not grant licences for drugs, like the American

Food and Drug Administration, but decides which drugs should be provided to patients free of charge by the National Health Service. In 2001, NICE recommended that drugs prescribed in the early stages of Alzheimer's should be used as standard, but in 2006 it changed its position and said they should only be prescribed on the NHS to people in the moderate stages of the disease. The drugs can be purchased privately, but older people, especially those on fixed incomes, and who have paid into the state system all their working lives, see this as unfair. This decision was challenged in court in August (2007) by the Alzheimer's Society and two pharmaceutical companies, but the judge ruled in favour of NICE.

NICE's argument was that the drugs, which cost £2.50 a day, were not good value for money. The Alzheimer's Society said that evidence from patients and their carers had not been given appropriate weight by NICE. NICE saw the drugs as cost-effective only in the moderate (second) stage of the disease because they delayed the need for care in a nursing home – care which, in many cases, is funded by the state. And the only treatment for distressing behavioural symptoms in late dementia, Ebixa, will no longer be available under the NHS.

NICE said its decision was based on the results of a five-year study, paid for by the NHS and not the drug companies, that found that the drugs are a 'waste of the scarce resources available for the condition', according to lead researcher Roger Gray, director of Birmingham University's clinical trials unit.[10] But old age psychiatry consultant, Roger Bullock, said the study was flawed in its design and execution.

Many experts spoke out strongly against the High Court ruling, saying that the decision 'beggars belief'.[11] Professor

Susan Benbow, of the Royal College of Psychiatrists, said: 'NICE itself said these drugs are clinically effective but they said they are not cost effective so they do not think they should be funded for people in the mild stages. This is a terminal disease in which people deteriorate until they die. What other disease would we say you have to deteriorate with before you get any treatment?' Dr David Anderson, chairman of the faculty of old age psychiatry at the Royal College of Psychiatrists,[12] said: 'The decision by the High Court is bitterly disappointing. I am astonished that the NICE process has been found to be rational and without perversity in this case.'

'The difference in my life was outstanding,' said an Alzheimer's sufferer. 'I was given my life back, albeit changed. From sitting zombie-like all day, I started to be glad to wake up. I saw things in colour again, I could make conversation with my family, and I could now choose for myself the right clothes to wear. Such joy, such simple things, all courtesy of two little tablets a day.'

Writing in *The Daily Telegraph* when NICE first announced its decision not to fund the drugs in October 2006, Jenny McCartney said

> The test of a morally civilised country is that it does things not because they are popular or easy, but because they are right. In its treatment of the elderly, Britain routinely fails that test. More money than ever is being pumped into the NHS, as the Government persists in telling us, and yet we have somehow ended up with a system that can apparently afford £1.5 billion a year to pay NHS management consultants, but not £2.50 a day for an Alzheimer's patient.

A related factor that is often downplayed in discussions of age-related health costs is that the cost of *dying* is more relevant than the cost of *ageing*

says Phil Mullan, author of *The Imaginary Time Bomb: Why an Ageing Population is Not a Social Problem*.[13]

The highest costs arise in the final six-to-18 months prior to death, whatever the age of death. Focusing on the costs of people with dementia in their final years forgets that this means we are paying the cost of these final months for fewer younger people – and in the context of dementia, 'younger' means people below the age of 80.[14]

The drugs NICE ruled out, Cholinesterase/acetyl-cholinesterase inhibitors, Tacrine, donepezil, rivastigmine and galantamine, are approved by the American Food and Drug Administration, though the medical system is different in the States.[15] The *New York Times'* Health Section (October 2007)[16] carried an informative article that began

Most drugs currently being used … to treat Alzheimer's are aimed at slowing progression. To date, none are cures. In fact, the improvements from some of these drugs may be so modest that even the patients and their families are not aware of them. Even in these cases, however, the drugs may delay the need for admission to nursing homes.

Even! Being able to continue living in your own home is a bonus for people with any disease, but especially dementia.

Disorientation is one of the major effects of dementia, and to be able to stay in familiar surroundings is hugely beneficial.

Family listening

As well as familiar surroundings, familiar routines are comforting to dementia sufferers. For Christians, 'quiet times', Bible reading, and Grace before meals are part of everyday life. Like tent pegs, they hold in place the fleeting fabric of the day, bringing a touch of the eternal and a sense of stability. In Pilgrim Homes, they give a sense of continuity and assurance, and are appreciated by residents and their families alike.

The daughter of one of our residents once told me that one of the things that reassured her was the way life in the home centred around the daily services.

'They create the structure and focus of the day,' she said. 'They happen right in the heart of the home and everyone is included. Because my mother couldn't talk, it was lovely sometimes to sit with her, holding her hand and joining in the hymns or prayers or listening to the readings. These short, informal services feel very natural; they are not a form of "entertainment" laid on by the staff but rather reflect a group of elderly people continuing their daily walk with God. And they provided the backbone, the meaningful rhythm to the day. Towards the end of mother's life, we asked for someone to read Psalm 23 (her favourite) to her. It was lovely, visiting one day, to find the Bible open by her bed – clear evidence of someone recently doing this.'

One of the loveliest articles published in our quarterly magazine was written by this daughter. It reflects the art, and the heart of listening so beautifully that, with her permission, I am including it here.

Glimpses through Dementia

It's 2.00 am. The telephone in our bedroom suddenly warbles and pulls us rudely out of a deep sleep. I fumble for the receiver and hold it awkwardly to my ear.

'I'm very worried about the pope,' says my father (a lifelong Anglican) at the other end of the line, *'he's been deliberately miscalculating the number of people living in Albania...'* *'Daddy,'* I reply, *'it's 2.00 am – the middle of the night!'* A pause *'Is it? – oh, I'm so sorry – but I thought you should act on the Albania situation while there's time.'*

I lie back on the pillow, all hope of sleep gone and prepare to let him tell me all about the Albanian situation but already he's moved onto other diverse topics. For the next ten minutes, international figures and personal friends move on and off a stage where the scenes change seamlessly from Albania to classic sailing boats to an imagined tea with the Bishop next Tuesday. Eventually, it's all off his chest and we can wish each other a gentle goodbye and God Bless and perhaps (on my part) a subtle reminder that most of the rest of his friends and family are sleeping right now. I replace the receiver and maybe could drift back to sleep but now my husband wants to know what the call was about and the process of reconstructing the ever-shifting story of popes and bishops and boats at sea along with the questions over the population size of Albania and who is coming for tea is a cognitive challenge which leaves us both wide awake – our minds buzzing with life's possibilities.

Sadly, both my parents, now in their 80s, have dementia and are in residential care. Their deterioration is a painful and bewildering process for them and for us but it is threaded, in and out, with some of life's greatest themes: relationship, identity, truth, life and death. And every now and then, we get a sudden glimpse of something humorous or puzzling or profound which we probably never would have stumbled across in more ordinary everyday life.

In my father's case, dementia has overtaken him suddenly after long years of the strain of looking after my mother. As a man who has long been a delightfully eclectic, whimsical and lateral thinker, always seeing life from a slightly different angle from anyone else, the expression of my father's dementia seems to reflect these identifying marks in the same way as a cartoonist's sketch first distils out and then exaggeratedly distorts the exceptions in someone's facial features. In his book, 'Consciousness Explained', Daniel Dennett talks of the mind being like a fertile pool where multiple thoughts and ideas are constantly bubbling up and competing with one another for attention. Our minds (when healthy) operate some kind of selection process so that we only express and use the thoughts or sentences which 'make sense' in the current context. In my father's case, it as if his ideas pool is bubbling as merrily as ever but the selection mechanism no longer operates the way it should. It is maybe the same for the rest of us when we dream.

When he is not distressed by his imaginings, then we find ourselves enjoying conversing with my father, playing with the strangeness of life and chuckling at the humour of the bizarre connections he makes. Did the Princess Royal *really* over salt the roast potatoes on Saturday night? And when you dial '123' for the BT Speaking Clock, does the clock on the bedroom wall *really* speak out the time? And how *do* you fit all the ideas you've had this week into a tight pair of socks? At best, it's as fun and refreshing as an excerpt from Lewis Carroll. At least, it reminds us how dull and restricting it is when we let our lives and views be over constrained by the actual facts, the rational explanations and the precise hour of the day.

The other thing we are learning through my father is that madness is not something so frighteningly 'other' and conversely, reality is not quite as solid as once we maybe thought. Indeed, reality may simply be what we choose to call the most common interpretation of any situation. That does not mean it is the 'right' interpretation or even the most useful, simply the one shared by the most people. We call some people 'mad' when their view of the world becomes sufficiently different (or challenging) to this 'norm'. We may call these people geniuses, but we may well reject their ideas to our detriment.

Even when my father phones us, distressed by some reality or other, his fears are not foreign. This is not foreign behaviour. If I pause and reflect, I can understand and relate to his distress.

My mother's decline has been a much slower and more gentle one; for her it has been like a slow descent into an ever-thickening fog which first clouded her memory and then her other senses and responses. Most days now, she is totally silent barely responding to our visits or attempts to communicate with her. But, every now and then, totally without warning, it is as if the fog clears for a moment in time and she will look at you and smile. Maybe she will reach out her hand to touch yours or say something to you – a charmingly prosaic remark which makes perfect sense in the context, for example, *'Please can you pass me that piece of cake?'*, as she points across the tea table. And, suddenly, there is this intensity of connection with her which, almost as you register it, has gone again as the fog re-envelops her. You find yourself looking around the otherwise empty room to convince yourself that the words can only have come from her!

One precious visit in October, the fog for some reason cleared for an entire afternoon and she and I lay on her bed and 'chatted' to one another in disjointed, spasmodic, but real exchanges. By the next visit, the fog had entirely closed in again and she looked straight through me once more. In the rest of life, it is possible to engage in many conversations of many words becoming careless of whether they make genuine connection or not. Communicating with my mother is now the exact opposite. It is entirely focused on finding a single phrase, a touch, a facial expression which will reach through the fog and make a momentary connection.

In contrast to my father, her pool of ideas and thoughts has slowly ceased to bubble but, when occasionally it throws something up, her selection process is still in perfect-operating form and only the appropriate sentence or gesture for the moment is expressed. How intriguing the mind is. When she occasionally smiles at my father or takes his hand, it may even be because she (unlike him) can tell that, whilst he may be able to talk, he is actually talking nonsense! An old friend who was visiting them one day was trying, at length, to correct one of my father's unfortunate 'misinterpretations' of the world when my mother (who had not uttered a word for days), reached out and closed the friend's lips with her fingers. As ever, she saw it as *her* role and no-one else's to shut my father up when necessary!

Before this all happened, I used to think (to the extent that I thought at all) that people died when their bodies stopped physically functioning. Life meant a beating heart. I am now slowly starting to recognise that the picture is much more complex than that. In fact, why do people with dementia die when they do? Maybe they die when their ability to connect with people, to sense the world around, to create ideas or to feel an emotion has totally gone – until then they are very much living and living the essentials of life. I don't know the answer, but I know that on this journey with my much loved parents, my naïve views on the great themes of madness, reality, communication, love, life and death are all being challenged to the core.

Listening to the end

The government acknowledged the importance of faith to the elderly in its advice to local authorities a few years ago.[17] It said that 'for older people from all groups, both majority and minority, religious observance is often central to their lives, but for minority groups living in a setting designed for the majority such observance may be difficult to achieve'. The advice was intended to highlight provision for ethnic groups (and the government does not consider Protestant Christians to be a minority group), but the principle is true. It's the reason elderly Christians come to Pilgrim Homes. All their lives have contained the detail and practices that are so important to them – morning prayer times, Grace at meal-times, Bible studies and worship services, as well as a code of living that sticks as closely as possible to the Scriptures.

One of our carers said that the energy needed to bring all the home's residents to the dining room was so enormous that sometimes she felt like lying down for a quick breather! But it is worth it, she added, because of the calming and comforting effect on the residents of just saying the Grace before the meal.

'You can see the calmness coming on them,' she said.

And sometimes, an individual who is not normally able to speak coherently will say the most beautiful Grace. One home manager said, 'Even when everything looks to the contrary, I am convinced that the Lord keeps His connection with us, through to the very end.'

CHAPTER 9

A Cup of Cold Water

'Carry each other's burdens, and in this way
you will fulfil the law of Christ.'
(Galatians 6:2)

Living not far from me is a couple in their early seventies. The husband has had a series of strokes and is suffering from vascular dementia. His wife, Barbara, has been caring for him at home for nearly two years, and is determined to do so until her, or his, dying breath, although she knows, in her heart, that there may come a time when he may need hospital or residential care. But their experiences of hospital so far have not been encouraging.

Formerly a successful businesswoman and not lacking in social skills, she was dismayed to find hospital staff distant and offhand. On one occasion she found her husband wearing a woman's pink nightie; when she managed to winkle a ward nurse out of the congenial staff huddle at the other end of the ward she was told, dismissively, 'We had to change his clothes and couldn't find men's pyjamas.'

She is not in the best of health herself. She has not had a full night's sleep for nearly two years, and every day she has to cope with his increasingly challenging behaviour. He will insist he is not dressed properly and won't settle until his clothes have been changed, usually more than once. He will repeat the same question over and over again, usually about her plan to run off with the man he believes she is hiding in the house, or is waiting just around the corner outside. The only time she has left the house is to step into her garden, which was always her delight. She can do this if her husband is content to sit in a chair in the doorway, which he will usually do to make sure she doesn't run away. Her life has become exhausting, debilitating and demoralizing; she looks dreadful. She is grateful for her family and friends, who visit regularly and help with the shopping, and in any way they can. Everyone who knows Barbara comments on how good they are to her.

Barbara is one of thousands of carers, including many older spouses, who manage to live, one day at a time, coping with a loved one with dementia.

'Some days I just wanted to crawl into a closet and scream,' wrote a caregiver in a Clarkesville, Tennessee newspaper.[1] 'One morning I found I simply could not get out of bed. The simple action of pushing back the sheet was too hard. I had nothing left ... My mother's brain is gone, but her body is like the Energizer Bunny. Keeps on going and going and going ... and I can't keep up. I'm so tired I am getting sick all the time...'

There are currently 689,000 people diagnosed as having dementia in the UK and only a third of them are in residential or nursing homes. The other two-thirds are being cared for in family homes, often by an elderly spouse. In America there are 4 million people with dementia, and given the value that American society attaches to family and grandparents, I wouldn't be surprised if the percentage being cared for at home was larger than in the UK. More generally, one in every four families in America now cares for someone over the age of fifty. A study for the Alzheimer's Society of Ireland found that for the 40,000 people with dementia, around fifty thousand carers are involved in looking after them, though the report did not say how many of those were in residential care or at home.[2]

The Irish study also showed that more than 60 per cent of carers spend fourteen hours a day, on average at least, caring for a person with dementia. As well as looking after the person with dementia, carers are the ones holding all the threads together; they are the key links with doctors, hospitals, community services and other relatives and friends. It is much more than a full-time job; it is physically, financially and emotionally draining and, unlike many other terminal illnesses, it can continue for years. Even when it has finished, the emotional aftermath takes its toll, sometimes years later.

In February 2007, BBC *News* interviewed Shirley Nurock, from London. Her husband, a doctor, was diagnosed with early-onset dementia in his fifties.

'At the beginning, he could do things and go out, and I could leave him at home on his own,' she said. 'And to begin with, I didn't think we could possibly need help. But each day a little bit of him went further away. Eventually I had to do everything with him. I had to stop working.'

Shirley was Leonard's only carer, every day for seven years. But eventually it became too much. 'Your life just disappears, your family disappears and your friends. You are left alone just doing the best you can,' she said. She contacted the Alzheimer's Society who put her in touch with social services, who arranged for a carer to visit for two hours, twice a week. Towards the end of his life, Leonard went into residential care, and died in 2003. In the interview, some four years later, Shirley said, 'You do not get much help from state services, and voluntary services are overstretched and pushed for cash. It made me angry and I am still angry now. Services are really fragmented. People with dementia are being rationed. It's criminal. It scares me for my own old age.'

In August 2007, British TV screened a documentary called *Malcolm and Barbara, a Love Story*. The film-maker became a new member of the family, filming alone with only a digital video camera. At the age of fifty-one, Malcolm had been diagnosed with early-onset Alzheimer's disease. The film followed them over a four-year period as Barbara became Malcolm's primary caregiver. Barbara became a campaigning member of the Alzheimer's Society, speaking at a 'Right to Care Symposium' in 2002, when Malcolm was sixty-two and in a very advanced stage of the disease. She was fighting a decision by the NHS to refuse to contribute to the high cost of Malcolm's twenty-four hour, seven-day-a-week care on the basis that it was not nursing care, but personal care – a battle that continues for thousands of others, to this day.

In a presentation at a conference in 2005, Hazel Levanthal, who cared for her sister, said,

'Once Alzheimer's makes itself known, it takes you into a battleground. From then on you have to fight; for a referral to a consultant, for a diagnosis, for medication, for benefits, for a care home, for help and understanding. Everything is such a struggle and there is very little guidance. When someone is

diagnosed with cancer certain strategies and treatment plans are set in motion – and there is a degree
of hope. Not so with Alzheimer's. It is as though the
sufferer and their carer have been thrown out into
rough seas without even a lifejacket to help keep
them afloat.[3]

Caregiver syndrome

To make matters worse, as Shirley Nurock found, carers
often find themselves isolated. It is not surprising that they
invariably suffer from stress, chronic fatigue, anger, guilt,
and depression. These symptoms are increasingly being
referred to as 'caregiver syndrome' by the medical community. Dr Jean Posner, a neuropsychiatrist in Baltimore,
Maryland, calls caregiver syndrome 'a debilitating condition
brought on by unrelieved, constant caring for a person with
a chronic illness or dementia'.

Caregivers, especially women, need individualized,
specific training in how to understand and manage the
behaviour of relatives and friends with dementia and how to
cope with their own feelings, said an article in the *Journal of
Advanced Nursing*.[4] Without training, and without a strong
community care system, most families and other carers are
hamstrung in their efforts to look after the person with
dementia at home. They must feel like Atlas, trying to
balance the world on their shoulders.

Caregiver syndrome can lead to high blood pressure,
diabetes and a compromised immune system. Peter
Vitaliano, a Professor of Geriatric Psychiatry at the
University of Washington, and an expert on care-giving, said
that in severe cases, it can even lead to death. Elderly carers,

particularly, are at a 63 per cent higher risk of mortality than non-carers in the same age group.[5] Professor Vitaliano likened exhausted carers' stress hormone levels to those of people suffering from post-traumatic stress disorder. Carers are usually so immersed in their role that they neglect their own care. The stress is related not only to the daunting work of care-giving, but also to the grief that comes with seeing the continuing decline in the health of their loved ones.

'Caregiver stress is directly related to the way our society views the elderly and the people who care for them,' he said. 'Today, care giving is viewed largely as a burden in this country. If it were viewed as more of a societal expectation and people were willing to offer more support, fewer caregivers would suffer in isolation.' What an indictment on a professedly civilized society – and what a contrast to the scriptural stance.

Carol Bradley Bursack, who has created a website for carers, sees another reason why caregivers feel isolated.[6] Referring to the 'caregiver syndrome', she commented

> Some of this stress stems from isolation and loneliness … but the carer often doesn't want to talk of burnout, for fear of sounding like a 'bad' person. So he keeps it to himself. Often, the short care-giving time that was expected extends into years, and by then the caregiver is so sucked into the routine of 24/7 care giving that he can't pull out. This self-neglect leads to a feeling of isolation and loneliness, even when the caregiver is surrounded by people.
>
> The simplest things can help. A couple of hours on the bicycle path, knowing that Mom is being watched by a trusted friend, can help the caregiver feel cared

for, thus breaking the downward cycle, for a time. An evening out with friends can refresh Sue enough so she can face another day without beginning it totally depleted.

The problem, of course, is in the nuts and bolts. Where does this relief come from? Friends may help in emergencies, but they don't look at your day-in-day-out care giving as an emergency. They see it as your life.[7]

In the UK, after a particularly sombre report of yet another NHS hospital failing elderly patients, one of our national newspapers announced a crusade called 'Respect for the Elderly'.[8] Recently it published an article by Ann Widdecombe, a well-known member of parliament, in which she contrasts the help on hand when her grandmother was looked after at home until her death, with the help available today. She recalled the final months when her grandmother stayed in bed

Her mind wandering, incontinent, all but paralysed by weakness. My mother nursed her, I carried trays up and down stairs and nobody would have dreamed of it being any other way. The district nurse called regularly and became a family friend. The doctor was kind and attentive.

Yet today, in a wealthier age, district nurses are stretched almost to breaking point with fewer and fewer caring for more and more. They are desperately needed by families where pensioner spouses or even pensioner children cannot turn patients, lift them or tend to intimate needs.

In time, my mother took on the task of looking after my father at home until his death. He was never the most easy tempered of men ... it would have been easy for mother to become isolated at home, but she belonged to an active church whose members supplied moral support. Today, many an old person goes for weeks on end seeing nobody.

When I was growing up it was still *de rigueur* to know the 10 commandments. The fifth is honour thy father and thy mother that thy days may be long upon the land which the Lord thy God gave thee. Our days will indeed be long, we of the post-war baby boom, but whether we shall spend them in a country that honours its elderly is much less certain.

Churches letting their light shine

'An active church whose members supplied moral support' has a wonderful ring about it. It would be a tremendous witness to a cynical world to see God's people helping to care for one another. Imagine the impact on our neighbours and colleagues! Picture the scene at the hairdresser, where the carer can relax for an hour, having her hair washed and styled. She could say to the hairdresser, 'Book my appointment for the same time next week, because someone from my church will be minding my mother so I can come'; to the doctor, 'Someone from my church comes and takes Mother out once a week, and a few people come with communion and to pray with her. She loves it and it gives me a little respite, too.' It wouldn't be long before people were saying, 'See how these Christians love one another...' Small touches can have such a big impact.

In the coming decades, as our population ages, churches have the opportunity to not only make a difference, and a life-changing difference at that, to members of their own fellowship, but also to do as Jesus said in Matthew 5:16: 'let your light shine before men, that they may see your good deeds and praise your Father in heaven.'

At a recent conference, I met someone from a church that had experienced problems with one of its long-standing members when she developed dementia. 'At first we could ignore it, or deal with it,' she told me, 'but it got so she was disrupting the service. When the pastor was speaking, for instance, she would say loudly, to the person next to her, "What's he going on about?" She used to be brought to church by her nephew, and she seemed to think a lot of him. So we decided to have a word with him. We explained that we couldn't think of anything else we could do other than ask him not to bring her to the services. He said he would bring her and stay with her, himself, and see if that made a difference. We thought that was marvellous, because he wasn't a believer. But he's been coming for three years with her now, and as long as he's there, she doesn't shout or disturb the service. And he tells us that he is enjoying the services!'

At the same conference I met a couple of people from an organization called 'Parish Nurses'. They are church members who are also registered nurses and will visit people to befriend and help them, not in a professional capacity, but 'coming alongside'. Their website is very informative, and gives contact details.[9]

Churches are having to get to grips with dementia. The more the population ages, the greater the number of older people making up our congregations. There are some fellowships that are already engaging with older people, but it would be good to see every church having a 'senior worker', as well as a youth leader, and an outreach leader. It would be in harmony with the Scriptures, as there are more references to older people in the Bible than there are to younger. I counted 194, and there are, no doubt, more.

Just a small group of people at church could make all the difference in the world to someone caring for a relative with dementia. Although the support of the pastor is essential, all he has to do is to float the idea; then a group will probably form and take things forward. There are usually willing people who need someone else to take the initiative. God will give the energy and resources needed. Some ideas for how people in churches can help is given in chapter 13.

Splendour

Conferences are a great place for meeting people, which is probably why people will fly halfway around the world to attend one. One of the most interesting encounters I've ever had was at a conference here in the UK at the famous Winter Gardens in Blackpool. When the sun was at its highest point of the day, it shone so brightly through the high domed windows (which had been installed to enhance its effect on the gardens that were once beneath) that those of us on exhibition stands in its path had to move to the shade on the other side of the hall until it passed over. When a bunch of extrovert evangelical Christians come together you get spontaneous church, and testimonies. We swapped our 'God stories'. They were enthusiastic about their reasons for being at the conference. I said that I was pleased by the warm response I'd received at our stand, because caring for the elderly didn't seem to ring bells for many churches. Then a young man, with a smile as wide as a banana said, 'You ought to come to my church. We've got a ministry for older people. It's run by older people too. We've got a minibus and we go out into the city to bring them in.' I thought the sun had gone to my head because, up to that minute, I'd never heard of such a thing.

A few months later I visited his church, in a rundown, inner city area in Bradford, Yorkshire. The church has nearly a thousand members, and I met a team of around twenty-five people, with ages ranging from the late teens to the mid-nineties. They were all enthusiastic and committed to reaching out to older people in their community, as well as caring for the elderly in their own congregation.

The oldest member of the team was 95-year-old Gertrude. She had been part of the church from its very early days, and had seen many changes. She told me her purpose in life was to encourage communication between the generations. She said, 'I can't do as much as when I was younger, because your body doesn't respond to what you want to do, though God does give me strength to do what I need to do. The church is such a blessing to me and to the young people. I am so happy to see them growing up and to know that when God calls me home the church is going to be all right. I am so excited about it.'

Gertrude makes a point of welcoming older people brought in by the minibus from care schemes in the area. Wheelchairs are catered for, and seats are reserved in the front, although people are free to sit where they choose.

The team is called 'Splendour', and is headed by Christine Chapman, who used to manage a residential care home. Christine is passionate about the welfare of older people, and is a lively 'champion' of their cause, enthusing young and old alike. Importantly, Splendour has the backing of the pastoral team. A few weeks before my visit, an 80-year-old man had committed his life to the Lord as the service came to an end. Delighted, the pastor said to the congregation, 'It's never too late! The devil thought all these years that he had this one safe in his hands. The devil thinks older people have no interest in the church, and then, at the eleventh hour, the Splendour Ministry comes along or some other ministry interested in older people and these people are giving their lives to the Lord. It's just amazing!'

As well as bringing people into the church, the church goes out to them, visiting care homes and sheltered housing schemes across the city. I watched a music group of young people practising some fairly lively choruses on keyboard, guitars and drums.

'Isn't that a bit foreign to older people?' I asked.

'No, they love it!' Christine said. 'They are just so pleased to have us there. We take in the Word and worship.' Then she added, 'But we do sing a combination of new songs and old songs, so they can feel they still belong and are part of the party. People get saved: in one home six older people gave their lives to the Lord.'

The length of the Sunday services means that they aren't suitable for all older people, particularly those suffering from dementia or with mental health problems, so the Splendour team created a ministry specifically for them, each Thursday. Every team member was excited about the project from the outset.

'We want to bring them in from all around the city, have a meal, and pamper them with massage and aromatherapy, hairdos and Bible discussions. We will have Word and worship and it's going to be purpose-filled and planned so people are going to feel really useful. People should not give up on life just because they are older. It's a different season of their life and we can plan for it and grow together,' Christine said.

Many teenagers in the church regard the older people as substitute grandparents, and it is a two-way appreciation. It's not just about old people; it's about the young and old coming together and being able to help one another. Some of the older people have mobile phones they're not sure of, and the younger ones show them how to use them. The oldest person to give her life to the Lord was a 100-year-old lady. There she was, a very new Christian, sitting next to someone who could be eighteen, who's been a Christian for ten years or longer.

Team member, 27-year-old Andrew Pollard, said he joined Splendour because he saw the older people had 'got it together'. He said, 'One of the reasons I am here amongst older people is because I realize that if I am going to be a great older person then I can learn from the older people who are around me.'

Christine took the baton of the work from Barbara and Paul Hargreaves, young at seventy-four and sixty-seven ('Although some might think we are elderly!'). Barbara and Paul had prayed that God would show them the right person to hand over to, someone with the right spiritual gifts and experience. Christine has years of experience in caring for older people and understands the difference between the culture of older and younger generations. She is one of those people with a natural heart for older people. She is happy to pass on the experience of the Splendour with anyone who would like to do something similar in their church. Splendour is not a denominational thing. Abundant Life Church in Bradford is not linked with a particular denomination, and the pastoral care it gives to the elderly is available in different forms for others, too, including carers.

The common element in ministries like these is the need for a champion, someone who will accept the 'commission' the Lord lays on his or her heart – and stick with it. One person can make a difference. Two hundred years ago, the commission to care for older brothers and sisters in Christ was accepted by one determined Christian, who became the founder of Pilgrim Homes. Despite initial opposition from the established church at the time, James Bisset's passion lit flames in others, and from a small group of supporters enthusiasm spread to dozens, then hundreds. The torch has been passed down from generation after generation of 'pilgrims', reinforcing the 'family in Christ' ethos that Pilgrim Homes enjoys today. Thousands of elderly Christians have been helped by the society since 1807, simply because one determined young man was passionate about helping older Christians 'who had been neglected by those of the same household of faith of which they are members and who are bound by the positive command of Christ and the nature of their calling to support them.'

In one of his talks, Roger pointed out that Jesus said, 'If you give a cup of water in My name ...' and 'what you do to them, you do to Me.' He added, 'We talk about missionaries who go overseas and we think – "To serve God is like that!" when Jesus said, "What I am actually looking for is people to give cups of water!"' (see Matthew 10:42)

It doesn't take a lot to offer a 'cup of cold water'; often it just needs the realization that someone is thirsty. And there are thousands of Christian carers who are thirsty out there.

CHAPTER 10

Sharing the Sufferings of Christ

'I want to know Christ and the power of His resurrection and the fellowship of sharing in His sufferings, becoming like Him in His death, and so, some-how, to attain to the resurrection from the dead.'
(Philippians 3:10–11)

Richard Taylor is a retired psychologist from Houston who was diagnosed with dementia in 2002, at the age of fifty-eight. He is one of the most outspoken advocates for people with dementia, and has written a book about its inexorable advance.[1] He says that people want him to describe 'What's going on in there.' Can he see the light flicker and fade? And there are those like him, other Alzheimer's victims, who want him to help their wives and husbands and children understand their reality. So he tells them what it's like in the first stage of Alzheimer's, and how it feels about being pushed into the second stage. There's a final, third stage of Alzheimer's. When that comes, Taylor says, he will be unable to describe it to anybody. Will anybody ever be able to describe it?

It is impossible to understand what it is like for people living with dementia in the later stages. Most of us know what it is to be temporarily disorientated. We can be on holiday, and wake up in the middle of the night in a strange room, look at the shadows and shapes of unfamiliar furniture and surroundings, and wonder where we are; then the haziness clears and we remember that we are on holiday. But we cannot imagine what it is like to live every day, uncertain about our surroundings, asking ourselves, 'Where am I?' The reason we want to know is to be able to help dementia sufferers better, to empathize with them deeply, and adjust to their capabilities. We want to see past the deficits, to the person. Getting to the core of the issue, or the heart of the person, takes empathy, patience and time.

Ngaire Beehre, a Christian home visitor in New Zealand, described a visit to a lady suffering with Alzheimer's.

Once when I visited June she was sitting in her chair crying. I knelt down by her and said, 'you're feeling upset today.' I took her hand gently in mine. She continued crying and I used a tissue to wipe her face, saying, 'You're feeling sad today, June. Can I wipe your tears? You're feeling really unhappy today.' The sobs continued as I stroked her hand, and said, 'there are lots of tears there. What are the tears saying?' I sensed a feeling of isolation and loneliness in 'my gut', so I decided to go with that and said, 'you're feeling lonely June, sad that you're all alone and nobody cares.' Her crying got louder and I stroked her arm to comfort her. 'It must be hard, feeling so lonely, isolated, all by yourself.' I continued strokering [sic] her arm. Her crying gradually subsided and she focused her eyes on mine. She gave a deep sigh. I continued to sit with her, holding her hand and stroking her arm. We sat quietly together and I was aware that I had entered her reality of distress and loneliness in some measure, bringing us to a position of relationship and mutuality. Then I continued our time together by reminding her, 'I'm Ngaire – I visit you.'[2]

These days there are a good handful of books written by people in the earlier stages of dementia that can give us an idea of the way it progresses. Jeanne is a lady in Hawaii who was diagnosed with Alzheimer's in 1995. As well as writing a book, she co-produced a local TV series with help from her doctors, friends and family: 'This series will reveal the thoughts and emotions of a woman struggling with a suddenly unmanageable life; numerous hospitalizations, suicide attempts, everyday turmoil and finally an extreme search for an accurate diagnosis of the illness responsible for it all. This woman is me, and I am living with Alzheimer's, not yet dying of it.'[3]

Laura Smith, the pioneer founder of DASNI, wrote

Most of the time I live in the space I can see and the time called 'now'. It is almost a 'virtual world' ... I move ... and a new space opens to view ... like a new room in a computer game. There is a type of cheese, I forget its name, that when thinly sliced is very lacy; my life feels like that – so full of spaces that it barely holds together, or like a tree in a gusty wind ... branches touch and connections are made but fleetingly, made and unmade, little sense of cohesiveness

... even my rooted-ness to my place in space feels tenuous, as if I might be torn loose, uprooted, blown away.'

In an interview in 2005,[4] Christine Bryden, the author of *Dancing with Dementia*, said she could remember the furniture in her mother's home from her childhood, but couldn't recall what happened yesterday. It is as if the more automatic something is for most of us, the more difficult it is for her. 'After I do something, the fog closes in behind me,' she says. 'I have to live in the moment. I am floating in time and space. I live in a little cloud ... but clouds have gaps in them – a bit of blue sky – moments of lucidity.' And what people with dementia say in those moments, Bryden stresses, 'is what they really think'.

The nearest I can get to imagining the final stages of dementia comes from a science fiction story I read years ago. Technology had made it possible for people to become integrated into their cars, which then became their virtual bodies. They lived most of their lives in their individualized bubble cars, which could feel, speak, hear and see. Final stage dementia could be like living in one of these little cars, where none of the controls is working, and there is deep fog on the inside. The 'eyes' still seem to be working, but sometimes the way the shapes move across the screen doesn't seem right. Nobody seems to be able to see me in here, and I can't communicate properly with them, out there. Things are unfamiliar inside, and uncertain outside. Even imagining this, I feel helpless, and very lonely.

Loneliness can be painful to see in individuals with dementia, even when they are surrounded by other people. Serita Washington is a senior nurse manager with Pilgrim

Homes, and a specialist in caring for people with dementia. Knowing how residents are cosseted in our homes, I asked her how they could feel lonely, when they are surrounded by such warmth and care. It's an effect of the brain disorder, she told me.

'While they are in this world they need human contact and interaction, and the disease has affected how they perceive that,' she said. 'Because of the trauma of the disease, sufferers feel lost; they feel separated from others and abandoned by them. We thank God that the Holy Spirit is comforting them, but being human, they still need people.

'Whenever she sees me, one of our ladies indicates that she wants me to go and sit and be with her and hold her hand. I take the time ... the paperwork builds up, but just to be sitting alongside her, to give that "cup of cold water" is very important.

'We try to keep them stimulated, too. We have conversations and activities, things that make them think, things they can join in like music, and keeping them involved as much as we can. We'll say, "I wonder what the weather is like out there?" and perhaps we'll go and walk through the garden, kicking through the leaves; we will listen to the rustle and crackle of the leaves, and crumple a few in our hands.'

As well as the specially trained staff in our homes, our residents are befriended by volunteer supporters drawn from local churches. There are three different types of support groups: one, the Auxiliaries, raises funds and publicizes the work in its region; another, the Home Support Group, provides pastoral support for the homes' management teams, praying with them, and arranging for people to take services in the home; and a third group, the Home Visitors, consists of people (again from local churches) who befriend individual residents, praying with them, taking them shopping and to the doctor's office, sitting with them, and becoming a friend and confidante. We would really like to have more volunteers like this, says Serita. 'The loneliness of people suffering with dementia is painful to see: I wish we had lots of volunteers, just to sit with them and hold their hands.'

Staff are trained in person-centred care in Pilgrim Homes, although in our case, it's like putting a cookie cutter over an already existing shape. It's what we have always done, with Matthew 25:40 in mind. When alterations or refurbishments are planned in one of our homes, our maintenance people will ask residents their opinions before beginning the work. After our home in Brighton had undergone a period of particularly gruelling refurbishment, which involved renewing the whole electrical rewiring system throughout the building, the manager, concerned that residents had felt unsettled, organized a 'Launch the Electrics' party, with the contractor officially giving her the key to the cupboard housing the mains control. Everyone entered into the spirit of the day, with the cook baking cakes that looked like various bits of electrical work. In another home, when the toilet rolls kept disappearing, carers discovered that one of the residents was putting them in a cupboard in her room. The manager decided it was easier to make the cupboard in her room a toilet roll store, with the resident 'in charge' of it, rather than upset her by taking them back.

Challenging behaviour

Not being able to talk does not mean not being able to communicate. Gestures, movement, facial expressions, all have a language of their own. A message is a signal from one person to another, with the meaning in the message, and sometimes you have to pay very close attention to what someone with dementia is trying to say when they cannot articulate it. Sometimes their frustration with not being able to communicate easily leads to agitation, and shouting. It is part of what has been termed 'challenging behaviour', though specialists like Andrew Papadopoulos, NHS consultant clinical psychologist, insist that there is no such thing. It is 'because behaviour is functional, largely indicative of inner meaning and the person's attempt to express their needs when they have lost their usual means of communication,'[5] he says.

The challenge to the carers is to try to understand the meaning in the behaviour, says Serita. 'There's always a reason for the agitation. We have to understand what's behind it. For example, one lady used to wear pop socks, and sometimes they would get tight, or not be pulled up properly. She couldn't bend over, so she would make this sort of moaning noise, or maybe rub her leg. We would bend down and release the pressure or pull them up, and she would be fine.

'Sometimes sufferers can resist when you are trying to help them, because they can't understand what you are trying to do. Or they may misinterpret you. You may be speaking slowly and clearly, just trying to make yourself clear, and they may be thinking, "This person is upset with me, they are mad at me." Some things they pick up wrongly. It's because of the harm done by the disease process itself.'

In another of our homes, one of our carers recorded

Night duty again, winter's night, doing a round, cardigan on. Mrs C. incontinent, so I fetch clean linen and get everything ready. 'You're not touching me, get out of my room,' she shouted, lashing out very aggressively and noisily. I go out, but know the job must be done. I wait five minutes and go back, removing my cardigan all ready for a confrontation and prepare myself for another onslaught. 'Hello dear,' she says, 'come in – I'm pleased it's you. You'll help me, won't you? I like you – you love me don't you, but don't let that one in the cardigan come near me, I can't stand her.' 'I know,' I reply, 'I don't like her sometimes, either!'

At the end of her report, Carol added a footnote.

You may smile after reading these short accounts. It's a good job I can see the funny side. But there is deep sadness within me, for these people. Think about the consequences of what is happening to these residents and to staff – feelings of inadequacy, worry and stress. But one thing we need above all else – LOVE.

Every step forward for a person who has dementia is a step into the unknown, and they can feel very insecure and frightened. Having someone alongside who is calm and loving makes a very big difference. Nevertheless, challenging behaviour can be demoralizing to carers who don't understand what is happening. A loving mother who gradually becomes totally silent; a church leader who now uses language that he has never uttered before; a likeable person who becomes difficult and unlovable. Families and friends ask themselves, *'What is going on?'*

In the past, people would come up with various theories. 'Repression' was one, thought to explain why some sufferers start to use swear words that have never passed their lips before; that the behaviour is due to sin in their lives that has not been confessed. The reason was thought to be that now that the person is weakened, the suppressed desire to swear – the unconfessed sin – is breaking through. This is not the case at all, Roger says.

'The Christian life is all about continual fellowship with God (see 1 John 1:5–6). A Christian is someone who has come to faith in Christ and has fellowshipped and walked with Him to the best of his or her understanding. It is true that none of us are without sin, for "if we claim to be without sin, we deceive ourselves and the truth is not in us." But the only people who are truly conscious of sin are Christians, and they constantly confess it. *It is not only cleansed – it is addressed by Christ.* The Spirit within us does not let sin lie unchallenged. We can refuse to acknowledge sin, or have a fear of facing it, but that points to our lack of coping, not to a lack of saving faith. Throughout our lives we are being formed in the image of Christ, and will only reach perfection in heaven.

'When Jesus died, He not only forgave our sins, He removed from God all recollection of our sins. He took away the entire wrath, anger and judgment that God has against our sins. Because of this there cannot be an issue of unforgiven sin, and there cannot be unforgiven sin, in a believer. There can be a failure to realize that sins are forgiven, and there may be a problem about needing to make restitution and resolve differences with others, but there is no such thing as unforgiven sin. Those who hold that abnormal behaviour in dementia is related to unforgiven sins have diminished the work of the cross and made a direct attack on the sufficiency of Christ's death. And those who grieve over past shortcomings, and even failure to "put things right", need to be pointed constantly to the cross. These are the facts of the gospel. So whatever is going on in the mind of a confused person, it is not the sin needing to be forgiven.

'The swearing is not because of a suppressed sinful desire – it is the disease. The brain records everything that we ever see, hear or do, indelibly, and it is because the illness has interfered with the brain's mechanisms that bad language is now being tipped out. Here is a poor confused person, who has been a believer all his life, but he is in a fallen world and dementia has hit him. Part of the impact of that terrible illness is this aberrant behaviour, and he has no control over it. It is not that he doesn't want to control it – it is beyond him.'

'Were you there, when they crucified my Lord?'

Some of the old, deep South's spiritual songs had meanings that stopped you in your tracks. On the surface, 'Were you there…?' makes no sense, because it happened nearly two thousand years ago. But in another sense, a very real one in the Spirit, we who believe in Jesus Christ *were* there. It is an amazing fact that everything the Lord did in His life – His sufferings, death and resurrection – involved us.

Jesus endured great sufferings and sorrows as He walked through this world as a man. He acted for us and we were represented when He did what He did. It is the central truth of Christian doctrine. And, in looking at the great truth of believers' union with Christ, the apostle Paul points to believers 'sharing in His sufferings' (Philippians 3:10).

In His life, Jesus suffered as our substitute and sacrifice, and these sufferings cannot be replicated by us. They are a once-for-all set of actions that secure our salvation. But Jesus' sufferings are also acts of devotion and commitment, in which He showed the extent and depth of His love to us.

In a similar way we suffer for Him in this world (Philippians 1:29; 1 Peter 3:14).

There is a further aspect of Christ's sufferings which we share – those which He endured because of the reality of His humanity and because of His living as a righteous man in a fallen world. It is in this area that dementia sufferers 'fellowship with Him'. (Romans 8:17; Colossians 1:24; 2 Corinthians 1:5–7). Christ's sufferings as a man living for God in an evil world are found in us who, because of divine grace and the indwelling Holy Spirit, seek holiness in a wicked environment.

'This was brought home to me in respect of Alzheimer's, when I was working in Birmingham,' said Roger. 'As part of my normal work, I visited a lady who was looking after her mother, who had very severe Alzheimer's. Her mother's behaviour had become so demanding that she needed support. As we discussed the situation, she explained that because of her mother's distressing behaviour at times, all her friends had stopped visiting. Although she was a long-term member of a large and very active church, neither the pastor, nor any member had been to see her for almost two years.

'At the close of our conversation I offered to simply read and pray with her (something I did not usually do then, because I was working for a secular organization). I read Psalm 41 and, as I did, she began to weep. She asked me who the psalm was about. I showed her that it spoke of the Lord in His last days (verse 9) and His experience of distress, desertion and isolation. "But that is Mum's and my experience," she said. "Does that mean that Jesus knows how I feel when I think of the condition that has afflicted Mum and me, and the way people have let me down?" I agreed, and just explained a little more how deeply the Saviour feels our distress and sorrow. Her smile of relief and even joy was amazing. She saw the "fellowship of sharing His sufferings".'

Some psalms graphically parallel this particular aspect of dementia – the horror and the sense of isolation that comes with the condition. Verses 9 to 13 from Psalm 31 describe how the sufferer is feeling: 'Be merciful to me, O Lord, for I am in distress; my eyes grow weak with sorrow, my soul and my body with grief. My life is consumed by anguish and my years by groaning; my strength fails because of my affliction, and my bones grow weak. Because of all my enemies, I am the utter contempt of my neighbours; I am a dread to my friends – those who see me on the street flee from me. I am forgotten by them as though I were dead; I have become like broken pottery. For I hear the slander of many; there is terror on every side; they conspire against me and plot to take my life.' How dreadful that a damaged brain can make a sufferer feel like this!

Yet, reflecting, as it does, the experience of the Lord as He walked to the cross, makes sharing His sufferings very precious indeed. The joy of knowing that Jesus knows and feels what the dementia sufferer and the carer are enduring is a great comfort. Paul says in 2 Corinthians 1:5 'as the sufferings of Christ flow over into our lives, so also through Christ our comfort overflows.' Jesus knew the pain of being misunderstood, and of loneliness.

'There's love and involvement and empathy that is so important. Sometimes all you can do is to hold the person's hand, speak respectfully and show affection. Sometimes you will weep with a daughter, a husband, a son... it's not a bad thing,' said Roger, 'it's a part of caring.'

A prayer, for people whose lives are affected by dementia

Gracious God, thank You that the Lord Jesus endured such sorrow and suffering that He might obtain our salvation. Thank You that He went more deeply into pain and anguish than we will ever go, when He took our place and died for our sins. And thank You that His experience of suffering and distress means that He fully knows what we have to endure and how we feel.

You know, dear Father, that to go through Alzheimer's disease and dementia is among the most difficult and sorrowful experiences of life. But You are able to strengthen and help us as we go through this pain. O gracious God, as we feel and know the suffering that Christ himself has endured, may we also know the wonderful comfort that His fellowship and fellow-feeling bring. Give us strength and peace of heart in the midst of the turmoil, that we may trust Him more, and prove the depth of His love towards us. Amen.

CHAPTER 11

Soul Talk

'a fierce-looking nation without respect
for the old or pity for the young.'
(Deuteronomy 28:50)

'Drink, eat and smoke too much: anything but grow old' was the title of a commentary in a leading British newspaper. The article proposed that dying early from an unhealthy lifestyle was better than living to a frail old age and having a poor quality of life. Describing the poor care many elderly people receive in hospitals and care homes in the UK, the journalist concluded that, 'Until the Government does something about it, I shall drink, eat and smoke myself silly, in the hope of going to an early grave. I'd much rather that than have to be elderly in Britain.'

In another article, columnist (and former editor) Charles Moore drew comparisons between people who sought to justify slavery 200 years ago, and those who vote for abortion today. Much as I like Charles Moore's columns, I would have skipped it except for the startling realization that the attitudes and behaviour he described are exactly the same as those affecting elderly people today. Two hundred years ago, people who were pro-slavery denied the humanity of the slaves, and today's pro-abortionists deny the humanity of the babies who are being aborted. Moore argued that today's technology shows that the foetus is a human being. He wrote

> The famous anti-slavery image was of a black man in chains, on his knees, saying, 'Am I not a man and a brother?' It was powerful because it used the physical to make a direct moral appeal: this person is essentially like you in body and soul, so why do you deny him the rights which you demand for yourself? To see a foetus in the womb is to experience the same appeal.

The tragedy begins when people are seen as objects, with either no humanity or an inferior sort.

> If you want to do people wrong, first undermine the idea that they are people. The Nazis called Jews rats ... pseudo-Darwinian views promoted ideas about racial purity or mental or physical health which allowed those who lacked these qualities to be seen as 'inferior stock'. One of the good moral trends of our time has been to reject this way of looking at things. Instead, we insist in the great debate about what it means to be human, that weakness is not a disqualification, but, by a famous Christian paradox, a strength.[1]

Although great strides have been made in promoting good care, the NHS itself admits that negative, ageist attitudes are ingrained in our medical services. Attitudes aside, practical provision is thin on the ground. Earlier this year (2007), half the nurses polled by the Royal College of

Nursing said there were too few of them to ensure that elderly patients in hospital were fed properly. Late in the year, shamed by press stories about elderly patients starving, the government announced a scheme have them weighed once a week, and their meals served on red trays to alert staff to their need for help. Even as I write this, I am finding it hard to believe, but it is true.

A 'malignant social psychology' was the phrase used to describe this attitude by leading dementia expert, Professor Tom Kitwood, in the early 1990s.[2] He said that it was characterized by treating people with dementia as children, intimidating and devaluing them, in effect, dehumanizing them. Kitwood believed that the biggest improvement for the quality of life of people with dementia came not from medical breakthroughs, but from recognizing them as individuals. There needs to be less focus on their 'deficits', and more on their needs as human beings.

In response, he introduced the concept of person-centred care, and spoke of the importance of 'personhood'. Person-centred care meant seeing the person as an individual, and not just a dementia-bearer. How far it has been adopted in practice remains to be seen; certainly my neighbour's husband would not have been wearing a woman's pink nightie if this particular hospital had been operating a person-centred care policy. If 'person-centred' is given more than lip service in our hospitals and care homes, we will owe Professor Tom Kitwood a deep vote of thanks. He died a few years ago, and is remembered with respect and affection by all who knew him. His work is being advocated by groups such as the Christian Council on Ageing Dementia Group.

How someone with dementia is cared for usually only becomes an issue when they have to go into hospital or a care home. When the person is being cared for at home, there will be years of shared memories, and there may be times when the individual 'clicks back' momentarily and those memories are rediscovered. Even where, as with Barbara and Malcolm, the couple in the television programme, the disease eradicates all evidence of the individual's personality, there will still be photographs and personal items all around, reflecting the life of the person before they became ill. It is when individuals have to be cared for by people who haven't known them before, and where they are in danger of taking second place to the treatment they need, that person-centred care is vital. If you think about it, even patients with all their wits about them find it hard to be treated as 'real people' in hospitals, instead of 'cases' taking up beds. It must be so hard for someone who is confused, and not able to express themselves clearly. Not all dementia sufferers will need to go into a hospital or care home but, when they do, their families will benefit by knowing that hospitals have guidelines regarding patients' care, and person-centred care should be among them.

Person-centred care in practice

When someone goes into a care home, a detailed care plan is drawn up. As well as medical, physical, and practical issues, the care plan covers the person's preferences as far as possible, gathering information from family and friends, as well as the individual. Carers will want to know their personal history, what matters to them and *why* it matters to them. In other words, all that has gone into making them the person they are now, and their unique make-up as an individual. We encourage people to fill in a Life History that will give us as full a picture about them as possible,

Jenny, a care home manager says, 'The more information you can gain about the person's past and present situation, the easier it is to see them as a whole person to be cared for, loved and respected. We ask family members or friends about their interests, hobbies, and past achievements. Each person has a past which has shaped their present life.'

Even apparently trivial things can make a big difference. For example, a couple of our homes have a cat, and residents enjoy having it around and stroking it. The cat likes the attention, too! Visiting one of our homes I saw how a resident with dementia liked to have the cat settle, purring, on her lap. This lady doesn't talk very much, but the pleasure in her expression said it all. Most people like cats, but not everyone feels the same way. One of my sisters is actually afraid of them, and if one should jump into her lap she would be terrified. When you are well it is a relatively unimportant detail, but if you have dementia and can't express yourself, your personal preferences take on much larger significance.

Mealtimes are important to the elderly in care homes. They form part of the structure of the day and are a time for socializing as well as eating. But older people can have very firmly held opinions about food. I once visited a care home and was impressed by the new cook as he enthused about the variety and changes he was introducing into the menu. We had lunch together with the staff team and his cooking was excellent. But when I talked to the residents later, they complained that the new cook didn't cook the vegetables enough; they couldn't mash them with their forks and, besides, they didn't 'trust' his sauces. When I said that overcooked vegetables lose their nutritional value, they replied that vegetables boiled to within an inch of their lives were what they were used to and that's what they wanted. As for his sauces, they thought he was covering up food they wouldn't like. I'm sure the cook quickly made adjustments, but it showed how important their personal preferences are to older folk. If someone with dementia doesn't like fish and can't communicate well, how can he let his carers know, other than by spitting it out? Their likes and dislikes are as important to them as they are to all of us.

We tend to take for granted our ability to affect the world around us, in small or large measure: we can make things happen, and make choices. It is linked to our feeling of being in control of our lives and to our independence. This sense of 'agency' is especially important to people with dementia. They do not want to be told, for example, that they must put on a coat before going outdoors in colder weather, any more than you or I would – this is how one speaks to a child, and is humiliating to *any* adult. A person-centred approach gives the choice to the individual and, using the coat in cold weather as an example, the carer will say, 'It's cold outside, and I'm going to put a coat on before we go out. What do you think? Would you like to put your coat on, too?' It is always giving the choice to the person, always asking, and never assuming. The same approach builds on what the individual can actually do, and encourages them to do it. For example, reading, praying, singing; helping around the home with dusting; anything that helps maintain a feeling of worth and well-being.

The key to really good, person-centred care is communication. Communication is much more than talking and listening, important though they are. Sitting silently alongside someone just holding their hand, as Serita mentioned earlier, says a lot to a lonely person. Smiling, laughing, your facial expression, the tone of voice, and the way you are sitting or standing, body language and making good eye contact are all important. Experts recommend touching, too, though you need to know the person well enough to know whether or not this is appropriate. In one of our homes was a very 'proper' 107-year-old, who had stern views about a number of things and, other than holding her hand, I can't imagine that she would ever have thought touching appropriate.

Going through a memory box containing significant mementoes can help in communicating. It's finding out what works best in connecting to the person with dementia. We've already observed how music and familiar choruses can be an immediate route to powerful memories.

Jenny, the care home manager mentioned a moment ago, adds how important it is to concentrate on the person; to listen intently and to think beneath the jumble of words. 'Gestures, cries, shouts and perhaps pinches – each person is trying to tell you something important. Listen to the words; watch facial expressions and body language for clues, because if you don't listen, the person will stop trying to communicate. Try to understand how things seem from their point of view. The world the person with dementia experiences is just as real to them as ours is to us. Encourage expressions of feeling through art, music, drama and poetry, Bible reading and prayer. Talk with them, not about them or above them. Never scold, mimic or patronize, but respect and promote the person's dignity. Treat them as you would want to be treated yourself.'

All human beings have a need to belong, to be recognized and to be accepted. Care homes are little communities, and individuals need to know they are a valued part of it. God designed each one of us to be part of a family throughout our lifetime, and helping the person with dementia feel that they belong lessens their feelings of isolation and loneliness.

In the last year, two Christian magazines in the UK have carried articles giving advice on what to look for when choosing a care home for a parent. To my astonishment, neither mentioned spiritual support, or the elderly parent's faith, though the authors professed to be Christian. Nonplussed, I emailed both editors, one of whom knows me slightly, but neither replied. It confirmed my growing real-ization that most people under the age of fifty do not have the slightest idea of how vital spiritual support is to the elderly. I've referred to this already, but it is so important that it's worth stating again. When you are older, and frailer, you need *more* of the Lord, not *less*. You won't fully realize this until you reach this point yourself, but people who work with elderly Christians will tell you how true it is. One of our longest serving home managers, in answer to a question about the need for homes especially for elderly Christians, said, 'Their faith has been so important to them all their lives, but they become so uncertain about *everything* as they grow older and frailer. Spiritual support means so much to them. You can see the difference it makes to them in devo-tions, and when you talk with them.' With this support, and the affirmation of their value to God, old age can be a particularly blessed time, and you can see this in the con-tentment they show. Perhaps Bunyan's *The Pilgrim's Progress* should be read at regular intervals in a believer's life: it is one of the few books that describe the fierce battle for faith as people near the 'Celestial City'.

It's worth mentioning that not everyone who reaches old

age will develop dementia and not everyone who develops dementia struggles with fears and anxieties. Many become quite content and happy. They suddenly become far more content than they have ever been in their life, as though the condition has somehow worked in another way. Even for these contented ones, spiritual support is essential for their well-being. There is a sovereign God at work, and He knows what people can cope with, and bear.

What to look for when choosing a care home

We are often asked how to choose a care home but, apart from some general, common-sense principles, it depends on the person concerned and what is important to them. Earlier this year, I helped arrange respite care with a local authority for a relative, and the year before, did the same for an older Christian with Parkinson's disease.

For the Christian gentleman, I helped select a local home that advertised itself as 'Christian', but was dismayed to find, when I visited him, that apart from the word 'Christian' on the name board outside, there was nothing else to show faith of any sort – not in conversation with the carers or manager, in texts on the walls or books on the shelves. There was no Grace said at mealtimes, no daily prayer times, nor visiting speakers. Sam (as I will call him) was the only Christian there. As it happened, Sam was delighted. An ardent evangelist, who used to take the train just to witness to the other passengers, he had a wonderful time with his captive audience. But Sam was comparatively young, in his sixties, and still mentally robust. When older and mentally frailer, he would only be able to fully relax in a home where his values and practices were shared.

My relative went into a local authority care home, which deserved a five-star rating. Staff were accessible, warm and caring, and made me feel as much at home as my relative. It was on a par with Pilgrim Homes, but without the Christian ethos. It suited my relative down to the ground, because he is not a believer.

When it comes to choosing a care home, charities like Age Concern and Help the Aged in the UK give excellent advice, and local authorities' social services departments are very helpful. I found in America that care homes and assisted living schemes are very open and helpful about what they offer. My son's father-in-law lived in a friendly, well-run assisted living scheme in Sun City, Menifee, and it was a pleasure to visit him there. But as far as I can tell, in any part of the world, what is not so easy to find is a care home where the Christian life is fully and naturally engaged, day by day.

For 200 years, Pilgrim Homes has been a 'by faith' society, not given to much publicity, and these days when we go to Christian conferences and exhibitions people are surprised and delighted to find that homes like ours exist. There are other Christian care providers in the UK, with excellent facilities, but as far as I know we are one of only a handful of *undenominational* Christian providers with homes *especially* for older brothers and sisters in Christ. It is these shared values, and the sense of all being on pilgrimage, that makes the atmosphere in our homes so distinctively Christian.

At an exhibition one year, we were asked by someone from an evangelical organization for permission to come and preach the gospel to our residents. We told her that in our homes it is the other way around – our residents preach the gospel to our visitors. Our Wellsborough home still has fond memories of Reg, who used to delight in nailing temporary contractors by their ears at every opportunity. Reg also mailed everyone in the local telephone directory with the same surname as himself, with the gospel message. Another resident used to catch the bus regularly every Wednesday to join a group of Christians witnessing in the town centre. He always wore placards, back and front, and when he didn't turn up one week, the bus driver leaned out and asked the waiting line, 'Where's John 3:16 today?'

Person-centred care in a hospital

On a ward with twenty to thirty patients with dementia and, say, six nurses, practical issues will take priority and there may be little time to spend with individuals. There is frequently not even time to make sure they are eating their meals. However, hospitals have guidance on the principles of care, and these should be in evidence.

People with dementia should

- always be listened to
- not be abused physically, psychologically or socially
- be spoken to kindly, as one would expect to address a senior and respected member of society.

1) They have the right to
- the same sources of healthcare provision as anyone else
- a secure and safe environment
- a good diet, which includes help with eating
- expect relaxation and recreation.

2) They should be able to
- express their views about the service
- make choices
- have an independent advocacy – that is, someone to represent them and speak up for them
- expect first-class care that satisfies them, not the carer.

3) They have the right to
- express their individuality
- satisfy their individual taste
- have their own clothes and belongings.

4) Their caregivers should
- receive appropriate professional support
- be supplied with all the information they need about dementia and the services available, with referral to helping agencies if necessary.

If one of my relatives developed dementia and needed to go into hospital, I would enquire about the hospital's guidelines for caring and whether or not person-centred care is in place. I would speak to the nurses in charge of their care, and make sure they had as much information about my relative as they needed. If possible, I would put up a 'life-board' with photographs of my relative at different times in their life, as Sir Cliff Richard did for his mother and as we do in our care homes. I would ask if there was anything that I could do that could help. We need to pray, too, for our hard-pressed nurses and medical staff, and show our appreciation for all they do.

Apart from the practical issues, the real principles of care, whether in a day centre or a residential home, or in a hospital ward, spring from appreciating the value of the individual, and it's both interesting and encouraging to see that 'best practice' principles of care are those that replicate scriptural values. The Bible makes it clear that God values human beings, so much so that He put them in charge of His beautiful earth. He does not regard us as objects, to be seen dispassionately. There are so many verses and instructions about valuing one another that it would need a whole book to record them separately.

CHAPTER 12

What's Happening to Grandma?

'Carry each other's burdens, and in this way ...
fulfil the law of Christ.'
(Galatians 6:2)

I used to think that it was a peculiarly English trait, when faced with someone behaving bizarrely, to react by pretending that nothing unusual was happening; to look the other way and hope the person, or people, will go away, quickly.

I was winding my way through crowds of shoppers, students and bicycles in Cambridge one day, when suddenly a clear path appeared as if by magic, and along it came striding a young man, barefoot and without a stitch of clothing. The amazing thing was that everyone on the street behaved as though nothing untoward was happening. He might as well have been invisible.

'How English,' I thought.

Then I saw almost the same scene in Munich, when (again) a young man walked through a café and into the street, and the only thing on his body was the radio he had pressed against his ear. The reaction from the people in

Germany was the same as those in Cambridge: they ignored him and he might as well have not existed. Would it have been the same in, say, Italy? America? Dubai? I think, in the anonymous populations of any large town, the reactions of the adults would be the same – the young man would be ignored. It would be partly out of embarrassment, but largely because we do not know how to cope with people who are obviously mentally unwell. Not only that; we know so little about mental ill health, other than depression, that we find it frightening. Charities such as MIND (The National Association for Mental Health) in the UK are working hard to change these attitudes with information and public campaigns, but there is still great ignorance about mental disabilities. It means that to change attitudes towards elderly people with dementia, there is a double barrier to overcome – first, ageism itself, and then the stigma attached to mental ill health.

Had there been children in either of those crowds (and there weren't, because it was during the school day), little questioning voices would have been heard ringing loudly and clearly. Children do not ignore 'the elephant in the room' and, if something is amiss, they want to know the reason why. Yet, paradoxically, in family settings, as long as children feel safe and loved, they seem to be able to cope with odd behaviour from familiar adults that would make others feel irritated, or uncomfortable.

There was an example in the television news coverage of the flooding in New Orleans, in 2006. Emergency services were evacuating people from second floors and roof-tops but, despite the danger, some were refusing to budge. One of the most obdurate was a retired headmaster, who was determined not to leave the house he had built himself and had lived in for forty years. He sat in a rocker on his second-floor veranda, with a jaw set like granite. Two of his grandsons rowed over in a small boat to persuade him, followed by one of the ever-present TV news crews. The old man would not listen to reason, so one of the grandsons climbed up, hefted him bodily out of the rocker and over the banister into the waiting arms of his brother in the boat bobbing in the water below.

Turning to the TV cameraman, the grandfather grumped, 'The only reason I'm going is because they're bigger than I am.'

With a grin, the grandson said dryly, 'He's an ornery critter, ain't he?' But it was clear that they had a deep affection for each other, orneriness and all. Had they been questioned, they would have said their grandfather's behaviour was not all that mysterious, because they knew him: they knew his history and understood that he didn't want to leave his precious house and possessions to the mercy of the floods and the looters; they understood, too, that for the old man it would be like letting go of a big part of his life that held deep meanings. They knew the hinterland to their grandfather's behaviour and words, and for them, he was behaving entirely in character.

Children, especially young children, and the elderly seem to communicate on the same wavelength at times, but when a grandparent starts to behave out of character, children will need explanations. So, what do you say to them when they ask, 'What's happening to grandma?'? And unlike adults, who will ignore embarrassing behaviour until it affects them personally, children will ask sooner, rather than later.

A lot depends on the closeness of family relationships, and whether the grandparent is part of an extended family in the main home, living in their own home, or in a care home. Children and teenagers will experience a whole mix of emotions, and the advice that experts give is good for everyone involved – the key is openness, and good communication. Encourage children to ask questions and give them simple and honest answers, without 'sugar-coating' the message. Teach them as much as you can about the condition, and reassure them that just because a family member has dementia, it does not mean that they, or anyone else in the family, are going to get it too.

Changes in someone with dementia, such as memory losses, are small at first and children will adapt to them. Forgetfulness, in small ways, is something everyone experiences and can identify with. It is when the forgetfulness increases and is accompanied by strange behaviour that the problems begin. Even then, children can be very forgiving of grandparents. I heard recently about a granddaughter who was almost inconsolable when her grandmother died of Alzheimer's. Tracy had been very close to her grandma, who had looked after her a lot when she was a child. Her grandma had loved to sing, and Tracy still remembers the childhood songs they sang together. She remembers the first signs of the disease, when her grandma began to forget things, and the day it became clear that she couldn't even remember her own children, including Tracy's mother and Tracy herself. But, even though she didn't seem to know who they were, she did seem to recognize them as familiar, and friendly. Tracy's grandfather looked after her grandmother until she fell and broke a hip and had to go into hospital. She had always been a lively character and, although the disease had stripped away much of her personality, one thing about her never changed – she still loved to sing. She sang the whole time she was in hospital, until just before she died. Tracy said she had never known such intense pain as the grief she felt after her grandma died, and would give anything to hear her singing once more. There was no hint of rejection when her grandmother didn't recognize her. Tracy accepted that it was the disease and she knew her grandma well enough to know that, had she been well, she would never have rejected her. She and her family continued to spend time with her grandmother even when she didn't know who they were any more. They were impelled by their love for their grandmother, and each other.

You might hear someone say, 'What's the point of going when she doesn't know who we are?' The point lies in the answer to 'Who are you doing it for? Is it for yourself, or is it for your grandmother?' There is something of great relevance for Christians, here, for there are two things that go deeper than understanding. The first is the Holy Spirit, who communicates in ways we will never grasp this side of heaven, and the second is love. Love always protects, always trusts, always hopes and always perseveres. Love never fails. Who are we to deny the power of love for one that needs it more than ever?

And does it matter that she's forgotten your visit the moment you go through the door? You have taken with you the Spirit of Christ and have touched the Spirit within her. Every story in the Bible is there for a reason, and we are told that when Elizabeth heard Mary's greeting, before they had had any conversation, Elizabeth's baby 'leaped in her womb, and Elizabeth was filled with the Holy Spirit' (Luke 1:41). Believers are bearers of the most powerful means of communication imaginable. It's worth mentioning again that one day Grandma will be walking around in Glory, and maybe

166 COULD IT BE DEMENTIA?

then, when we know and understand everything, you will realize how important your visits really were.

Good communication

Prepare children for changes, knowing the condition will get worse over time. This progression can be very hard for them, because the grandparent may look physically well, and just the same they always have, and they need to understand that although the individual may look fine on the outside, on the inside their brain is not working as it should. Explain about the brain being the bridge of our physical 'ship', and the individual's controls now becoming damaged. Tell them that thousands of people are suffering from the same condition, and scientists are working hard to find a cure, though it may not be in time for their grandparent. Let them know that people with dementia still need to know that they are loved. They want the same kind of reassurance you would give a child – or anyone for that matter – a hug and a reminder that God loves them too. Say that inside, in their heart, Grandma or Grandpa still loves them, as they always did, but just doesn't know how to show it because the controls aren't working.

Sometimes a person with dementia will behave angrily or fearfully towards the child, and they need to know that the grandparent did not mean to behave like that – they are not doing it deliberately. ('The hardest thing of all, which made my sense of injustice boil and rage, was being judged on behaviour for which I was not responsible, over which I had no control,' wrote someone who suffered brain damage after a stroke.)[1] Children can feel bewilderment and fear because they don't understand what is happening; sadness, because the beloved grandparent is changing; frustration, because of having to repeat things when they are not being understood; then guilt for getting angry; and unsettled, because they are not sure how to behave around the grandparent. Let children know that it's not their fault. You can explain that people with dementia have good days and bad days, like the rest of us, but the children are not responsible for the bad days.

Dementia brings a series of losses, which can be like little bereavements – the 'long goodbye' that Nancy Reagan mentioned. It is harrowing enough for adults and can be traumatic for children. They may become withdrawn, or lose patience, or have a physical pain like a stomach ache or headache. They may become stressed, and their schoolwork may suffer. They will have many questions: 'Why does Grandma call me by my mother's name?' and 'Why does she keep asking the same question?' and 'What's happening to Grandma?'

The most powerful antidote to pain, confusion, guilt and fear is the presence of the Holy Spirit. Ask Him to comfort the children. Remind them that although it is a very sad time now, one day their grandparent will be with Jesus, and He has promised a great reunion for all those who believe in Him, where everyone will be together again, in perfect health (1 Thessalonians 4:13–18). Make sure that in family prayers, as well as individual prayers with the children, you thank the Lord for the promise of the new heaven and the new earth, and for the life of the grandparent. Read the scriptures about how all our bodies will grow old, and wear out (2 Corinthians 4:16–17), explaining that the brain that is not working properly is part of our physical body, but that the grandparent's soul, the spirit of the person, is intact, and being comforted by the Holy Spirit in a way we can't understand. Children haven't built up the mental complications that adults often have and they expect to be heard, and answered in prayer. Indeed, Jesus said that we need to have their childlike ability to believe to be able to enter heaven (Mark 10:14). Ask your pastor, or church elders, to include the grandparent and family in public prayers, too, because that will help normalize the situation for your children, and assure them that, even though their grandparent is 'acting weird', other people still care and know that it is the illness that is the problem, not the person.

Give the children tactics for coping, so they don't feel completely helpless. (The same tactics are helpful for others to know, too.) Show them how to use short, simple sentences and give frequent cues and reminders, especially as to time and place. For example, 'It's twelve o'clock now, Grandma. You had a nice breakfast earlier. Would you like a cup of coffee now, here in the kitchen?' Explain that now that Grandma's short-term memory is poor, they can help her feel comfortable by talking about events that happened long ago. Give them some prompts, some memories of your own they can use, and perhaps some photographs. For example, 'Do you remember the day I fell out of the apple tree, Grandma? Look, you put a plaster on my knee.'

Show them how to use targeted questions that can be answered with just one, or a few words. A long answer may make Grandma feel embarrassed and frustrated because she can't hold the words in her mind long enough to give a long answer, and only having to give a short answer can help her feel successful, more connected and 'with it'. For example, instead of asking, 'What did you have for breakfast today?' try, 'Did you have bacon for breakfast this morning?' Explain, too, that dementia sufferers can seem to be slow to understand, or speak, or respond, say, when asked to come into the dining room. When this happens, encourage them to be patient and repeat the request: 'There's no rush, Grandma. When you're ready, we'll go into the dining room.' Tell them not to pop up suddenly in front of Grandma, or to go around the side of her, because that would frighten her and she may lash out. Always make sure she can see and hear you approaching. They need to know, too, that Grandma is happy just to have someone sitting with her, in silence. Teenagers often like loud music in the background, but tell them that too much background noise can be confusing for Grandma, and it's better to have a quiet background for her.

The essence of helping people with dementia is patience, and love. Grandma may say to one of the children, 'Help me', but may not say what she needs. Show the children how to handle this but, first of all, how to orient Grandma in time and place, asking questions, again, that only need short answers – for example, 'Are you cold?' or, 'Do you have a pain?' or, 'Shall I fetch Mum?' in case she needs help to get to the lavatory.

It can be difficult to make sense of what Grandma says at times, because she is commenting on something that is happening in her world, not ours. A friend told me about her elderly aunt, who, a day or two before she died in hospital, told her that earlier in the day her husband had brought in an empty suitcase to pack her clothes and take her home in the morning. The husband had died several years before, but the friend wisely did not argue, and her aunt died peacefully, shortly afterwards. She had been so happy with her husband's 'appearance' and promise, and what would be achieved by trying to argue with someone whose reality is so different to ours? If Grandma tells the children, 'I want to go home', it may not mean that she wants to go back to the house she used to live in; it may mean that she wants to feel comfortable and safe, as she used to in the past.

The more involved your children are with helping in daily family life, including helping Grandma, the better able they will feel to cope, because it strengthens their sense of 'agency'. And if Grandma is used to having children around, they will be part of the world she can relate to. There may be practical things you can do together: perhaps having one of the children write reminders for Grandma on an A4 sheet and pinning it up where she can see it; or making a memory box, and a life-board. They can pin up favourite pictures on the board and put in notes, or mementoes about the favourite times they have had with Grandma in the memory box. They can also include scripture verses, and poems, or prayers.

We are hearing more today about the 'sandwich' generation: those parents who are raising their own children and, at the same time, having to take care of their own, aging parents. The pressure is very great when a parent develops dementia.

'Potentially, dementia affects the next generation, that is, the children of dementia sufferers,' said a typical 'sandwich' parent. 'We're caught in the middle. Here we have our teenagers going through all their problems. Then we have our elderly parents with their problems. It's up to us to sort things out, and to keep the balance. These things often happen; as one generation is going through something, then another one needs you. I feel very pulled in two directions.'

Looking after someone with dementia is not just time consuming – it is *all*-consuming. It drains your emotions, your energies and your finances. It would be so easy to overlook your children's needs. So keep an eye on them and try and set time aside to spend exclusively with them – real 'quality' time where you can engage fully with them and give emotional support. Getting away for a day, or even half a day together, and having a break, will help ease the pressure. Perhaps a friend, or another relative, or someone from the church could take over for a little while. There may be support groups near you, or a day centre where the grandparent could be looked after for a while. Most blessed of all is if you have an active church that takes seriously God's commandment to love one another and is already coming alongside your family; perhaps one or two people from church could sit with your relative, while you take time out. Even a walk through the mall or a coffee at McDonald's together is a great, refreshing treat, when you have such continual pressure at home and, as a caregiver, you need to take breaks as often as you can. In reality, that may mean not very often!

Many people say that keeping a sense of humour is very important. One lady told me, 'My sisters and I find it helps to laugh about the funny things that happen. It actually helps to laugh or we would have to cry.' This can be true for the children, too. Children love to laugh! As long as it doesn't become cynical, and they always laugh with the person, not at them.

It's worth mentioning that, although you may not get so many people offering to help that you have to organize a rota, it is important to accept offers when they're made. You could even make a list beforehand, in a quiet moment, so you are prepared when you are asked. On one of the occasions when my grandson, in South Carolina, was rushed into intensive care, as we were coming out of church that Sunday, a group of ladies gathered around my son asking what they could do to help. They knew that Tomos's mother was staying in the hospital with him, and they asked Hywel, 'Can we come and clean for you? Can we do some gardening? Shall we cook some meals? Can we do some shopping? What can we do?' My son was so preoccupied that he refused every offer, and one of them even pleaded, 'Can't we even clean the fridge for you?' He still declined, because he didn't have the mental capacity, at that moment, to allocate tasks and manage what needed to be done. But I could see that the church ladies were grieved. They really needed to feel that they were doing some good, even in the tiniest way; it was their way of showing that they cared. If someone from church offers to help when you are coping with a relative with dementia, bless them and grasp the offer with both hands. This is, not least, for the sake of the children, as it will give you more time for them. You could even give your pastor, or a church leader, a copy of the list.

Two-thirds of people with dementia are currently being looked after at home by relatives. You may be one of the caregivers. Hopefully, your doctor has told you about the help that is available and someone from your local social services has visited you. But the time may eventually come when you cannot manage any more and part of the equation may be the welfare of your children.

After a long struggle, one mother said, 'We tried to have my mother live with us as long as possible. It was the children who had trouble coping. They would wake up in the middle of the night to find Grandma standing by their bed. She had no idea of where she was supposed to be and she couldn't tell whether it was day or night.' The children would wake up the mother, who would put Grandma back to bed, usually more than once. No one was getting a good night's sleep and we need sleep if we are to cope with life, even at the best of times.

In a 2005 Gallup poll of 1,000 adults over the age of fifty, less than a third of those surveyed (32 per cent) reported getting a good night's sleep all seven days of the week. And yet, they ranked good sleep as more important even than interpersonal relationships. Dementia sufferers often sleep poorly and night-time can be a disturbed time for everyone in the household. It can be the last straw. There is also the issue of keeping a balance between the needs of the children and those of the person with dementia.

In his pastor's role, Roger listens to caregivers, and sometimes has to tell them that they are coming to the point where they cannot manage at home any more. He says, 'A verse in 1 Timothy, chapter 5 says, "If anyone does not provide for his relatives, and especially for his immediate family, he has denied the faith and is worse than an unbeliever." Sometimes people take that verse to mean that you have to keep being the provider of care for your relative, come what may. But what the verse is actually saying is, "It's the responsibility of Christians to make the best provision for their relatives, and it's up to them to decide what that provision means." My wife and I look after my wife's father, and we had to make the decision that we couldn't look after my mother in our home, so we found what we thought was the best care home for her, and it proved to be so.

'So many people try and struggle through by themselves. We all have a ministry to help each other, and we need to find loving and gracious ways of helping them to make that decision. Then, when they have made it, to help them live through the result. After giving so much care, and being so caught up with the needs of the one with dementia, life can seem very empty for those left at home, and we need to help them through it. We need to stay in touch with them; to visit, and telephone, to let them know we are thinking and praying about them.'

In summary – how best to help children cope:

- As soon as the diagnosis is made, obtain copies of litera- ture giving information about the disease, not just for yourself, but to give to your children, relatives, friends and your church.
- Be open, and completely honest about what is happening to the individual with dementia. Do not try to protect children by 'sugar-coating' it.
- Build a memory box and life-board for – and as far as pos- sible with – the person with dementia, involving other members of the family.
- Encourage children to remember Grandma (or Grandpa) as they used to be, and remind them that one day they will be perfectly whole, with the Lord.
- Pray together, and try to keep a scriptural perspective on all that is happening.
- Make sure that children do not feel that it is their fault when Grandma shouts at them, or is angry with them. Remind them that although Grandma looks just fine, inside her brain is damaged. Grandma still loves them.
- Encourage visitors by reminding them of the ministry of the Holy Spirit, and the power of love, even if they feel their visits are unfruitful.
- Let children know it is natural to feel frustrated by having to repeat things, and then to feel guilty.
- Give them tactics for coping – short, simple questions, and how to give frequent cues and reminders. Tell them, too, that silence is all right.

- Tell them that Grandma needs a quiet background, as too much noise makes it difficult for her to concentrate.
- Remind them that Grandma's world may seem very different from ours, and not to argue with her when she says something that is wrong, because it is real to her.
- Tell them not to pop up suddenly in front of Grandma, because that would frighten her and she might lash out. Always make sure she can see and hear you approaching.
- You need to take short breaks with the children. Find out if there is a day centre near you, or what other facilities there are. Ask friends and relatives for help. Sometimes people are too proud to ask for help, but you need to do it for your children's sake.
- Write a list of things people can help you with, in advance of being asked. Give the list to your church pastor, or leader.
- Ask your pastor to pray for your family and for Grandma, openly. Others may continue to pray on their own.

CHAPTER 13

Serving One Another in Love

'His intent was that now, through the church, the
manifold wisdom of God should be made known to the
rulers and authorities in the heavenly realms.'
(Ephesians 3:10)

It is an all too familiar story. Jane was married to Brian, a considerate, gentle man for many years. At the age of fifty-nine, he began to have fainting fits at work. A brain scan showed that some of his brain cells had died, and he retired straight away.

Without the stress of work he seemed to be all right for a few years, but then he began to have quite serious memory losses, and would forget things from one day to the next. A visit to a neurologist showed that he had Alzheimer's, and he was given Aricept, which helped for a few years. But then, things seemed to go downhill quite quickly. He would flare into awful fits of temper, and hit Jane with his fists. He found fault in everything she did, and she began to think that perhaps everything was her fault – that her inability to cope was making him lose his mind. He seemed to hate her so much that he delighted in making her miserable.

At church one morning he had a fit and, after that, his driving licence was revoked, which meant giving up his last vestige of freedom. He became angry and bitter, and his behaviour deteriorated even further. He even threw his food on the floor. Jane says they had an excellent GP, who used to visit, but, apart from him, there was no support or advice. Life became such a nightmare that one morning, as they were sitting in the kitchen, Jane said she wanted to turn on all the gas rings so they would go to sleep, and end it all. It was their lowest point, and prompted them to make decisions about what they should do. That night she prayed for help, and it came swiftly and unexpectedly in the form of a lady whose mother was suffering from Alzheimer's. She introduced Jane and Brian to the Alzheimer's Society and, from then on, the help they needed began to be put in place.

It is sad that the doctor who visited did not point the couple to the resources available, and in mentioning the church, the inference is that there was no support from there, either. Why did no one visit, the subtext seems to say, or even take the trouble to find out what help was available? Just imagine how different the couple's story would have been had they been supported by their church.

Roger remembers giving a talk in a church where the pastor said afterwards, 'I realize there's a lady in my congregation who hasn't been for two years because her husband has dementia. I don't think I have visited her in two years. I feel terribly guilty and I know nobody in my congregation has visited her in two years.'

It's not that church members are cold-hearted and indifferent – it's just that most are not aware of one another's needs. I truly believe that if we loved one another as Jesus commanded us, our churches would be packed each Sunday and I wouldn't be writing this book about how to help people with dementia. Shelves in Christian bookshops would be groaning with the weight of books on the subject by pastors and elders – and we wouldn't have stories like Jane and Brian's. The Alzheimer's Society would be coming to us to ask about the spiritual aspect of caring for people with dementia.

One of the best examples of pastoral care is in my former church in Cambridge. When I go back I feel as though I've never left. The worship music is not a performance but draws everyone in; the teaching is sound and the Holy Spirit is not quenched. Although it is a large, growing church, there are home-group meetings each week, and everyone seems to look out for one another quite naturally. A few years ago, the church moved to a fair-sized building so it could include facilities for the local community that would let them show Christian care, and it is now looking for an even bigger building in order to do more. It seems to have plans for helping almost everyone you could think of – except the elderly. I shall probably have to wave a white flag when I visit after this is published, but it's true. It could be because the church's stated mission is to reach the younger generation and, until quite recently, there have been few older people in the church. But I believe that folk there are so keen to please the Lord in all things that if someone were to propose a pastoral care programme for older folk, it would be supported by the leaders. It's just that as far as I can tell, no one has seen the need for it yet. Care for students, for mothers and toddlers, for people with addictions and those needing counselling, yes – but for the elderly, so far, nothing. And I suspect that's how it is with most churches.

Yet there are shining examples, like the ones in Yorkshire, and undoubtedly others that I haven't heard of yet. There are signs, too, that the big ship is slowly turning, and that God is beginning to turn the rudder, imperceptibly. Some friends took me to a church in Dudley, England where I heard an Anglican vicar, Mark Stibbe, speak about a powerful change in direction the Lord had given his church. They had been planning to buy more land and spend well over a £1 million on building a bigger church – a *much bigger* church, and Mark decided to take a few months out beforehand to travel to really big churches to see how they worked at ground level, so to speak. The more churches he visited and the more pastors he spoke to, the more unsettled he felt. The witness in his spirit about the *really bigger* church grew ever more discordant, until he realized that God was saying, 'I don't want you to build a bigger church. I want the church to be doing what is uppermost in My heart – looking after widows and orphans.'

But Mark had a problem. The people involved in the project were firmly focused on it. How could he tell them that God wasn't interested and had different priorities altogether? A planning meeting was due, and Mark prayed, feeling decidedly apprehensive. (If Nehemiah and Esther were watching from heaven, they must have been nodding in sympathy.) The day came, the meeting took place, and the outcome was agreement that their resources, financial and human, would not go into a building for a really bigger church, but into helping widows and orphans. Listening to Mark, I wished that instead of being in a church in Dudley, we were all in a church of a type in the States where the congregation responds vocally to the preacher, and I could have stood up and shouted, 'Yeah man! You got it right, man!' The

Reverend Stibbe came close to being hugged by a perfect stranger. I am praying that God will take more church leaders 'out of their village' (see Mark 8:23) for a while, to speak to them about the widows and orphans.

There are plenty of churches helping orphans, of course, and thank God for that. But when it comes to widows and the elderly, *especially* those belonging to the family of God, there is very little. Could it be that we expect mature adults, especially Christians, to be self-sufficient and independent? That is not how the Bible sees it.

'God did not design human beings to be independent,' explains Roger. 'Independence is something that has come out of the world of psychology. God himself is a trinity, and the trinity is a mutually dependent being. You cannot think of the Father without the Son, and the Son does not function without the Spirit, and the Spirit is the Spirit of the Father – and God made man to be like himself, to be a dependent being. God designed us to live in communities, and that's why "family" is the core concept in the Scriptures. Independence is a fallacy, and just because someone needs someone else's help, it doesn't mean they are less than human. It means that God has designed them to have the privilege of being served by others, and others have the privilege of serving. We are created by God to be mutually dependent, and to serve, and be served. It is a gift of God to be served by His people.' The Bible tells us to 'serve one another in love' (Galatians 5:13) and the church in the Scriptures even kept lists of their widows, to make sure they were not overlooked. Writing to Timothy, Paul said Christians who do not care for their elderly relatives are the same as infidels (1 Timothy 5:8), developing the theme of the fifth commandment.

Serving one another seems to have disappeared from our

current Christian discourse, at least, among evangelicals. If you take a broad sweep across our Christian media today you will find nothing about serving one another, even less about serving the elderly. Yet the Bible has a lot to say about the importance of older saints to God. How much clearer could He make it than 'Rise in the presence of the aged ... and revere your God. I am the Lord' (Leviticus 19:32)?

In the past, evangelical Christians have led the way in caring for others. It is a part of our Christian tradition. Many of the caring institutions, such as education, the hospice movement and nursing care were initiated by Christians. In the 1880s, a time of grinding poverty and early deaths, especially among children, one of the great social reformers was Lord Ashley, the seventh Earl of Shaftesbury. He introduced several acts limiting the hours children could work in factories and coal mines. He also cared about elderly Christians, and was a keen supporter of our charity, speaking publicly on Pilgrim Homes' behalf. In 2007, the world celebrated the day the British parliament passed the bill outlawing the trans-Atlantic slave trade. It was the beginning of the end of global slavery, and the end of a twenty-year battle by another evangelical Christian, William Wilberforce. Passionate about the value of each individual to God, he became vice president of Pilgrim Homes in 1824, staying in post until his death in 1833. Nowadays, slavery is seen for the abhorrence that it is; but in the early 1800s it was simply a fact of life.

What churches can do

If you are a pastor, your first thought will probably be – *I can't do another thing!* But the only thing you need to do, really (if you haven't already), is open your heart to the need.

You have the resources, and they just need to be released. God has promised that you won't find yourself over-burdened. 'God is able to make all grace abound to you, so that in all things at all times, having all that you need, you will abound in every good work' (2 Corinthians 9:8). Try it!

Most of the work in any organization is done by only a percentage of the people, and the majority of its resources lie untapped. It's called the 80/20 split, or the Pareto principle, after the man who first defined it – 20 per cent of the people are active, and 80 per cent are passive. The 20 per cent are usually very, very busy, and the 80 per cent are not. There's a picture of this in 1 Samuel 17. There, on the one hand, stood the ranked mass of the Philistine army; row after row of armed men, ready for battle. Standing opposite them was the army of the Lord. But instead of the armies engaging, they sent out their biggest, most powerful champions to fight on their behalf. The armies themselves were behaving like spectators and cheerleaders. It was a terrible strategy. The Israelites were passive, and looking at the giant, Goliath, they forgot the size of their God. The longer they did nothing, the lower their morale plunged. Then God showed His glory by sending in a young, untrained lad who was on an errand for his parents, bringing lunch for his brothers. He didn't look like a mighty warrior, and he probably smelt like a sheep, because minding sheep was his job. But David had a different mindset to the others, and he saw straight to the root of the matter – that the battle wasn't about fighting for territory or about which champion was the strongest, but was a direct satanic challenge to the God of Israel.

You may think I am stretching the analogy here, but isn't ageism and the dreadful indifference to the Lord's elderly saints a similar challenge to the God who treasures them?

Isn't it the inevitable result of Darwinian thinking that says they've had their day; that they're now on the downward bend of the evolutionary cycle?

Perhaps we need to encourage the Davids in our congregations. Often a 'good work' begins with a suggestion from people in the congregation. This is how an email prayer network was started – it grew in just two years to become the backbone of a church's prayer life. When retirees Gwen and Reg Stewart found themselves feeling on the edge of church life, unable to pray intelligently or go to prayer meetings because they couldn't hear what was going on, they suggested setting up a weekly prayer requests email network.

'And guess who got the job?' Gwen said. 'Our church prayer network has been going for over two years now. Each week praise/prayer requests are sent to us for us to collate and email in time for the mid-week prayer meeting. These can be about anything – health, gospel opportunities, family or work concerns, Christian service in the church or outside ... The emails are confidential to church members and regulars. Currently we send to over a hundred email addresses (including our own overseas missionaries) so a larger number of individuals see it. Those who are not online get hard copies from others.

'This has been one of the most encouraging things we have been involved with for a long time. As far as we personally are concerned, it keeps us in touch with a lot that is going on (though some things we still don't hear about!) and, in a large, growing church, we have contact with people we would not otherwise see – we exchange emails with people we have yet to meet! It has been widely received and welcomed. Indeed, we have more positive and appreciative feedback from this than perhaps we have ever received from anything else we have done!'

When something works as well as this, it motivates the others, and so much is down to motivation. Indeed, if Mr Pareto could be persuaded to leave and take his split with him, then 100 per cent of the church would be available for a part of the action, even if some could take only a tiny part.

According to someone whose ministry involves motivating churchgoers across all denominations, the biggest reason for standing armies, and a lack of motivation, is that people feel inadequate. Martin Graham heads up 'On the Move', an evangelical ministry that reaches people by giving free barbecues.[1] The local church is mobilized, with something like 100 to 200 Christians from local churches taking part in each mission. Typically, over a hundred non-Christians are there at any one time, but over two hours, an average of 600 come along, and about two thousand turn up over three or four days. Hundreds of 'On the Move' missions have taken place in the UK and overseas, all involving volunteers from different churches. Thousands of people have given their lives to the Lord, usually joining the church of the helper who spoke with them.

When Martin visits churches to encourage helpers, he tells congregations, 'If I asked you to come and evangelize hundreds of perfect strangers, you'd probably say "No, I couldn't do that." But you could come and chop onions, and flip burgers, couldn't you?' It's about showing people what they can do, and recognizing the talents God has given them. It also means, as Martin found, keeping each job small, and clearly do-able.

So, instead of asking for volunteers to form a group to help a family caring for someone with dementia, which would have most of your congregation diving under the pews, you could focus on one small task, such as 'Could you look for information on the internet for someone caring for a relative with dementia?' Or, 'Could you give half an hour, once a month in a rota with others, to sit and hold someone's hand?' Better yet, because people are drawn to the flame of another's passion, is to find a 'champion', someone like Splendour's Christine in Bradford, who will hold all the ends together and organize a group.

God is so generous with His gifts that there is a huge amount of ability packed into even a small church fellowship. If you were to look around your church this Sunday morning, you would find talents that would answer almost every need. Think of the dozens of activities that fill our everyday lives that we do without thinking, but that pile up and add to the pressure on people struggling to cope. Mundane things, such as making a telephone call, doing the ironing, doing some shopping, picking up a prescription, cutting the grass, making a cup of tea, vacuuming a room, helping to fill out an official form, taking washing to the launderette or collecting the dry-cleaning, changing a light bulb, and so on. The whole of the alphabet doesn't have to be covered by one, two, or even three people! People will have their own likes and dislikes. And there truly is no accounting for tastes; I know a couple of ladies who actually love household chores – one even loves to clean the bathroom. You may remember a TV commercial where a young mother paid a baby-sitter so she could be free to escape for a few minutes and enjoy her hot chocolate, just for a few minutes... How much more will a break like that mean to a caregiver?

'If we are going to be Christlike, let's be practical,' Roger says, 'Christlike does not mean being really spiritual in a meeting. It is about not breaking bruised reeds, but means loving them, and helping to restore them. It's not saying to carers, "That's life, isn't it?"; it's loving and supporting them.' He is one of those rare pastors with extensive experience of dementia sufferers (including his own mother) and he gives some ideas for churches that he knows are 'do-able' and will make a difference.

Here are Roger's suggestions for churches who have folk with dementia in their midst.

When the individual with dementia is still in church

- Bring together a group of people who are happy to be involved. Support and encouragement cannot come from one individual on their own. Involve everyone in the planning and in working towards the same goals. You may want to consider organizing a workshop for members of your group. In the UK, specialists from Pilgrim Homes take workshops with church groups.
- Find out from their caregiver as much as you can about the person. You may know them to an extent from your previous relationships in church, but to help them when they are less able to communicate means knowing more than you did before.
- Give the caregiver the telephone numbers of people in the support group, with an indication of what they are able to help with. For example, the ladies who like housework, the tall teenagers who will change a light bulb, the men who will cut the grass, the person who can help with difficult form filling and approaching different organizations for help, and so on.
- Start practical activities as early as possible, so the person with dementia gets to know people who are giving

support, and the carer can get a break. This will stimulate and help the sufferer and, at the same time, relieve the carer.

- Stress the need for sensitivity and understanding. People with dementia may need more time to express themselves. It is important that everyone understands this. A small delay in anything doesn't matter to people without dementia, but may be significant to someone with dementia, who may have different priorities – something to bear in mind when arranging a ride for them to church.

- Have members of the group sit alongside the person with dementia in church. How they behave and speak with the individual will be 'role-modelled' to others in the congregation, making them feel better able to relate to them, too. This will avoid the individual feeling that they are being avoided.

- Consult with the person about 'ground rules'. Ask the individual whether there are any ways that meetings could be made easier for them – for example, sound levels, or hymn books or Bibles with large lettering, or sitting nearer the exit for the toilet.

- Consider organizing a special 'club', or day, as the Splendour team did for people with dementia in their area of Bradford. It could include arts and crafts that stimulate the mind, aromatherapy that is relaxing and pleasant, and special, short services that involve them. Think about involving the young people in the church. The aim is to enable individuals to be part of the life of the church.

- In conversation – don't worry if the individual makes no reply. Be sensitive, but keep talking to encourage responses. Speak to them with respect – the mind may have failed to a degree, but they are still fully human, and created in God's image. Speak clearly, and look directly at them when you are talking. Don't be afraid to make jokes and laugh, and don't worry about tears, but comfort and be natural.

- In church, pray publicly for suffers and their caregivers, for they are a part of their fellowship. Pray for their real needs – for comfort and peace of mind; ask the Lord to be real to them.

- Pray for them as you would 'normal' people, which is what they still are; pray for God's grace in their lives; pray that the Spirit may make Christ real and pray for true Christian experience.

- Help to 'bolt on' resources. Churches are not expected to do things they are not skilled at doing, such as medical care, or professional nursing, but they can help by knowing what is available, and helping the family obtain it, sometimes by helping to fill in the relevant forms.

When the individual is being cared for at home

- When visiting them at home be a good friend, showing real interest and concern; keep occupied with whatever they enjoy doing; help them do practical things, such as bits of cleaning, simple gardening, painting and drawing, pottery and plaster work. Some people love animals, so, if the carer thinks it is a good idea, bring a dog along, or pet their cat.

- Talk about normal things – about things they did and like; about people they know, especially family; talk about what is happening at church, so they still feel a part. Their long-term memory will be stronger than their short-term, so talk about the past, prompted by photographs, pictures, objects, postcards or news items. Just one example of stimulating the individual's memory would be to talk about weddings they have attended.

- Don't talk loudly, as we British tend to do with foreign language speakers – and don't argue or try and interject with your reality when they say illogical things – for example, when an 85-year-old says she is going to see her mother. Try and bring the person back to reality in a gentle and sympathetic way, but don't argue.

- Take the dementia sufferer out for a walk, or to places they knew well and might remember.

- Organize communion for them, and take extra people along. Sharing communion can be a deep touchstone for believers. I don't believe we fully understand the depth of this sacrament.

- Play music, a tape or CD with familiar hymns, or play an instrument. When old hymns are played, they may be able to sing along, or tap a foot. For most there will be a light in their eyes as they remember that Jesus loves them.

- Talk much about Christ and the Bible. This is probably the best thing of all. We know from our residents that deep calls to deep and the Holy Spirit communicates to the person's spirit. Speak much about the cross, the centre of faith and the Spirit's work; speak about heaven and the future.

- Pray that they may be ready for heaven, that God would keep them from sin. Pray that they may be spared undue sorrows and suffering.

- Pray with them and encourage them to pray. Pray clearly, but briefly.

For those who are now living in care homes, or on EMI (Elderly Mentally Infirm) wards, in hospital

- Organize frequent visitors from the church. It helps the person, and gives a wonderful testimony to staff and others.
- As staff advise – take the person for a walk, or on trips, remembering that even a short drive around the block can be different and exciting for them.
- Sit with them while they participate in the home's or the ward's activities.
- Speak positively about their circumstances, and support staff – unless there is something clearly wrong, and even then do not involve the person in the issue.
- Pray for the home or ward staff; pray for other residents and patients.
- Pray that the individual may settle and be contented; pray that relatives may accept the situation, because often a relative's disquiet communicates itself to the sufferer.

For carers, while the individual is still at home

- Be there for them in practical ways, being there to support, not organize. There is a time and place for 'taking over', but not so that the carer feels a failure in any way.
- Offer to help with cleaning, shopping and maintenance of the house and garden. Even taking on a small chore, like going around to put the trash bins out on the right day, can be a great help.
- Take the dementia sufferer out for a while, to give the carer a break.

- Arrange a sitter for the sufferer, and take the carer out for a few hours alone.
- Find out if there are any opportunities for, or arrange, a carers' group, while the individual is meeting elsewhere, so they can share feelings and fears. It is so important to keep the carer involved in church life.
- Talk normally about everything – let the carer set the agenda but encourage them to be open about their feelings and fears. Guilt and anger are common among caregivers, and are powerful, often hidden, feelings that need to be expressed. Let them know that it is legitimate to have these feelings, as long as they are not nurtured. Pastors and leaders can arrange to provide more specific support and counselling.
- Talk normally about the sufferer and their condition – talk about the practicalities.
- Talk much about spiritual things. Personal devotions can suffer when there is someone to care for. Encourage spiritual thought and delight, being positive and hopeful; share personal readings, both from Scripture and other books.

For the caregiver, when the person with dementia is no longer at home

This can be a time of deep emotions for caregivers, when they are left to struggle with a sense of failure, and dreadful loneliness.

- In practical ways – help with transport and attendance at the care home or hospital. Ask what help is needed in daily tasks.

- Ensure regular visits – watch that loneliness and depression do not set in; take the carer out on trips, shopping expeditions and fun things; make sure they stay involved in church life and activities.
- Talk about normal things: feelings of guilt and concern about the sufferer now being looked after elsewhere; and, if possible, talk sensitively about the future, and even death. Remember, Christians have a different view of death from those in the world.
- Pray for the carer, including prayers for the home or hospital, for the staff, and for the future.

When the Holy Spirit was in the prison of a body where the brain was damaged; when someone couldn't communicate; when they forgot how to eat and needed to be fed – He will know those who cared for Him.

The principle of Matthew 25:35–40 is crystal clear. People suffering with dementia need exactly the help the Lord describes in these verses. I like to think of Him, when they meet face to face, saying to the people who have helped care for His precious pilgrims with dementia, either directly or through their caregivers, 'You did it to Me.'

CHAPTER 14

This is Our Day!

'A gray head is a crown of glory;
It is found in the way of righteousness.'
(Proverbs 16:31, NASB)

A large part of any pastor's ministry is to encourage the saints, and Roger has a special ministry to those who are further along their pilgrimage. This chapter is not about dementia, but is to encourage our older brothers and sisters in Christ. As for who is old – we leave that to you to decide. Roger writes

> I was talking with a friend some time ago about a major Christian event he was involved in organizing, and I was asking why it was structured in the way it was. I had made the point that I felt a significant number of older people who had been long-term supporters would feel excluded and alienated. He looked at me and, with utter sincerity, said, 'But older people have had their day!' I was shocked, disturbed and not a little hurt for some older people who were standing nearby and overheard what was said. Of course, what shocked me most was the utterly unbiblical nature of his thinking.

I thought about that incident recently when I was reading Luke 2:25–38, the stories of Simeon and Anna at the time of the dedication of the baby Jesus. It is a wonderful picture of the importance and ministry of older people.

Delight in Christ and anticipation of heaven

Simeon shows such wonderful appreciation of the Saviour. He had a special understanding about the child. But what is so special is that despite his advanced age (and everything in the text leads us to think he was pretty old) he was so full of the Holy Spirit. What spiritual vigour and sensitivity he had because of his communion with God and the presence of the Holy Spirit upon him. He was just so full of his God and the salvation he was providing. And because of this, what a blessing and source of illumination and strength he was to that young couple, Mary and Joseph.

We may not have the same privilege of ministry and prophetic insight he had, but we can be daily 'filled with the Spirit' (see Ephesians 5:18–21), and we can be a source of instruction and encouragement to younger people. Indeed, that is part of the specific calling for every older person (Psalm 71:18; Psalm 92:12–15). What great things about God we have to tell and how others would be blessed if they heard our God-centred stories. Like him, we can have that godly longing for heaven that means we talk about the hope within us and we get excited about God's promises. And that is infectious and stimulating to others. I have known so many older people who loved to talk about the glory, whose joys were all in heaven. I always go away from them longing to be there myself, and that helps me to resist sin and be a little more holy.

I guess Satan would have been so much happier to hear Joseph say, 'But older people have had their day.' But for God and for Simeon in his old age, that day when a young couple with a baby came into the Temple *was* his day. Simeon delighted in Christ and had an eager anticipation of heaven, and so he was a blessing.

Full of prayer and encouragement

And then there was Anna. How old was she? At least eighty-four, and some would argue much older. Surely she had entered spiritual retirement? Not her! Full of 'fasting and praying', that was her life. Night and day she did it. She probably had problems sleeping – a lot of us do. But when she woke up in the night hours, she began to pray. It had become a holy habit so that even when she was not too well, she still prayed for others as well as herself. And throughout her days she prayed – probably not in big lumps of prayer; as we get older, our concentration slips and so we have to pray in short bursts. I'm sure that's how she did it. And then she talked to people about her hope, and the promised Saviour. Once she had seen Jesus, then that was her conversation. She told everyone she could that He had come. What an encouragement she was.

I have no doubt our heavenly Father looked on Anna with great delight and sent precious consolations into her heart. And as she prayed and encouraged others, the Lord worked out His purposes through her many prayers, and answered her urgent longings in remarkable ways. But can you imagine what was happening in the gates or council chambers of hell? There was Satan holding a special meeting to consider how he could keep Anna quiet – her prayers and her encouraging conversation caused him so many problems. But the Lord kept her and guarded her – she was serving Him.

And someone says about us older ones: 'But older people have had their day.' Here we are today and we seek to use our time – in the night and during the day – by sending up prayers, mainly short ones but some longer ones. And in heaven the Father is delighted and sends us consolations and answers. On earth the will of God is carried out, because that's what we pray about. And the devil is racking his brain to work out how he can stop all these older people praying so much and being an encouragement to others. But we are serving our God and He keeps us and uses us in a thousand unseen ways.

Had our day? Nonsense! *This* is our day. We will delight in Christ and anticipate heaven and share our joys and insights with whoever will listen. And we will pray and encourage others, and so God's will will be done. Older Christians, don't let anyone discourage you. While you have breath, this is your day – use it well.

Organizations Offering Advice and Help

In the United Kingdom

Age Concern

Age Concern is the largest UK charity working with and for older people. The website provides information about local branches throughout Britain. A national helpline will give links to local branches.
Telephone: 0800 009966
http://www.ageconcern.org.uk/

The Alzheimer's Society

The UK's leading care and research charity for people with dementia, their families and carers.
Alzheimer's Society
Gordon House
10 Greencoat Place
London SW1P 1PH
Telephone: 020 7306 0606
Fax: 020 7306 0808
www.alzheimers.org.uk
Email: enquiries@alzheimers.org.uk

Carer's Christian Fellowship

The Carer's Christian Fellowship aims to offer a link and support for Christians who are caring in some way for a relative, friend or neighbour. The Fellowship offers mutual support to fellow Christians by prayer and sharing the reality of the Christian experience in the middle of the stress of caring.

The Carer's Christian Fellowship

14 Cavie Close

Nine Elms

Swindon

Wiltshire

SN5 5XD

Telephone: 01793 887068

www.carerschristianfellowship.org.uk

Carers UK

Carers UK is the voice of carers. Carers provide unpaid care by looking after an ill, frail or disabled family member, friend or partner.

Telephone: 020 7490 8818

Carers' Line: 0808 808 7777

www.carersuk.org

Crossroads

Caring for carers.

Crossroads Association

10 Regent Place

Rugby

Warwickshire

CV21 2PN

Telephone: 0845 450 0350 / 0845 450 6556

www.crossroads.org.uk

DISC

Dementia Information Service for Carers. Advice and information for carers of older people with dementia.
DISC
Oxford Dementia Centre
Institute of Public Care
Roosevelt Drive
Oxford OX3 7XR
Telephone: 0845 120 4048
http://www.disc.org.uk/
Email: info@disc.org.uk

Help the Aged

Advice and support. Website provides information about local branches throughout Britain.
Telephone: 020 7278 1114
www.helptheaged.org.uk
Email: info@helptheaged.org.uk

PARCHE

Pastoral Action in Residential Care Homes for the Elderly. Meeting the spiritual needs of elderly people in care. PARCHE, together with Eastbourne churches, offers regional help. National training and envisioning for church teams.
www.parche.org.uk
Email: PARCHEenquiries@hotmail.co.uk

Parish Nursing Ministries UK

Whole person health care through the local church.
Reverend Helen Wordsworth
3, Barnwell Close

Dunchurch
Nr Rugby
Warwickshire CV22 6QH
Telephone: 01788 817292
www.parishnursing.co.uk

PDSG
Pick's Disease Support Group – Lewy Body Dementia
The PDSG charity is under the umbrella of the National
Hospital for Neurology and Neurosurgery Development
Foundation. Caring for people with frontotemporal dementia is hard; there are few facilities tailored for the younger
sufferer and those are not always appropriate for people with
frontotemporal dementia. Website provides regional links.
www.pdsg.org.uk

In the USA

Alzheimer's Association
919 E. Michigan Avenue, Suite 1000
Chicago, IL 60611
24/7 helpline – contact us for information, referral and support.
Telephone: 1–800–272–3900
Tdd: 1–866–403–3073
http://www.alz.org/
Email: info@alz.org

American Association for Geriatric Psychiatry
7910 Woodmont Avenue, Suite 1050
Bethesda, MD 20814
Telephone: (301) 654–7850

Family Caregiver Alliance,
National Center on Caregiving
690 Market Street, Suite 600
San Francisco, CA 94104
Telephone: (800) 445–8106
(415) 434–3388

National Alliance for Caregiving
4729 Montgomery Lane, 5th Floor
Bethesda, MD 20814

National Institute on Aging
Alzheimer's Disease Education and Referral Center
PO Box 8250
Silver Spring, MD 20907–8250
Telephone: (800) 438–4380
(301) 495–3311

National Institute of Neurological Disorders and Stroke,
National Institutes of Health
31 Center Drive, MSC 2540
Building 31, Room 8A–06
Bethesda, MD 20892–2540
Telephone: (800) 352–9424 (recording)
(301) 496–5751

National Institutes of Health and National Institute on Aging
An official US website with information and links.
http://www.nia.nih.gov/Alzheimers/default.htm

National Mental Health Association
2001 North Beauregard Street, 12th Floor

Alexandria, VA 22311
Telephone: (703) 684–7722
http://www.nmha.org/

Gerontological Society of America
http://www.geron.org/online.html
Gives a list of other organizations.

Mid-America Congress on Aging
Some different but interesting links, such as census data and
financial assistance organizations.
http://lgrossman.com/macareso.htm

http://www.thirteen.org/bid/resources.html
Website for a New York Public Broadcasting Service with
information and links focused on end-of-life care and issues.

International

http://www.alz.co.uk/alzheimers/languages.html
Page on UK Alzheimer's site with links for information in
many other languages and countries.

http://www.healthandage.com/html/min/adi/page2.htm#naa
This website has general information and also this page with
contact information for Alzheimer's organizations in various
countries.

International Federation on Ageing
IFA serves as an advocate for the well-being of older persons
around the world. A voice for older people globally.

Secretary General: Dr Jane Barratt
IFA
4398 Boul. Saint-Laurent, Suite 302
Montreal QC, Canada
H2W 1Z5
Telephone: 1–514–396–3358
Facsimile: 1–514–396–3378
www.ifa-fiv.org/en/accueil.aspx
Email: jbarratt@ifa-fiv.org

The International Parish Nurse Resource Centre
Reverend Dr Deborah L. Patterson
Executive Director
Deaconess Parish Nurse Ministries, LLC and
International Parish Nurse Resource Center
475 East Lockwood Avenue
Saint Louis, MO   63119
Telephone: 314–918–2527
www.parishnurses.org
Email: dpatterson@eden.edu

Notes

Chapter 1

1. www.faculty.washington.edu/chudler/worldaz.html
2. Information from the National Institute of Neurological Disorders and Strokes.
3. The National Institute of Neurological Disorders and Stroke.

Chapter 2

1. Lee Dye, Scientists seek Peronality's Roots in Brain, 27 June 2007, www.abcnews.go.com/technology/story?id =97961&page=1
2. '"God Spot" is found in brain', by Steve Connor, Science Correspondent, *Los Angeles Times*, 29 October 1997.
3. F.H.C. Crick, *What Mad Pursuit: A Personal View of Scientific Discovery*, (London: Penguin Books, 1990), p. 138; R. Dawkins, *The Blind Watchmaker: Why the Evidence of Evolution Reveals a Universe Without Design*, (New York: W.W. Norton, 1986), p. 210
4. www.faculty.washington.edu/chudler/plast.html

Chapter 3

1. www.en.wikipedia.org/wiki/Human_brain
2. www.st-andrews.ac.uk/news/Title,14097,en.html
3. www.agingresearch.org/content/article/detail/867
4. 'Alzheimer's Disease: Vascular Etiology & Pathology', Amos D. Korczyn, *Annals of the New York Academy of Sciences* 977:129–134, 2002.
5. Dr Oliver Sacks, *The Man Who Mistook His Wife for a Hat*, London: Picador, 1985, p 36.
6. www.fda.gov/fdac/departs/2007/207_note.html

Chapter 4

1. *Daily Telegraph*, 15 February 2007.
2. The joint report can be seen at www.healthcare commission.org.uk
3. *Archives of General Psychiatry*, February 2007.

Chapter 5

1. RSNA News, September 2005, p. 18: www.rsna.org/publications/rsnanews/upload/sept2005.pdf
2. Paulo H.M. Chaves et. al., 'What Constitutes Normal Hemogolbin Concentration in Community-Dwelling Disabled Older Women?', *Journal of the American Geriatrics Society*, September 2006.
3. *Neurology*, 28 August 2007.
4. Newhouse News Service, 12 September 2007.
5. www.medicine.ucsd.edu/ses/
6. By Amy Ellis Nutt, Newhouse News Service, published on 12 September 2007.

7. *Ashburton Guardian*, New Zealand, Wednesday 5 September 2007.

8. *Journal of Nuclear Medicine*, August 2007, Associate Professor Omer Bonne at Hadassah-Hebrew University Medical Center in Jerusalem, also www.news-medical.net/?id=28629

Chapter 6

1. She is the author of the books *Who will I be when I die?* (Christine Bryden, London: HarperCollins, 1998), and *Dancing with Dementia*, subtitled 'My story of living positively with dementia' (London: Jessica Kingsley Publishers Ltd., 2005).

2. *Dancing with Dementia*, p. 97.

3. www.neurology.org/cgi/content/abstract/59/2/198

4. w w w . o p e n 2 n e t / h e a l t h l i v i n g / b o d y - _mind/two_lifespan2.html

5. www.news.uiuc.edu/news/06/1120exercise.html

6. Archives of Nerology, 2006; 63:1545–1550 (E.J. Schaefer, et. al.)

7. *Vanderbilt Medical Center Reporter*, 1 September 2006.

8. *San Francisco Chronicle*, 14 September 2007.

9. University of Massachusetts Lowell, www.129.63.176.200/Media/News

10. www.news.independent.co.uk/health/article2586652.ece

11. *FASEB Journal* (Federation of American Societies for Experimental Biology), in September 2007.

12. The Linus Pauling Institute at Oregon State University, the University of Toronto, University of California/Berkeley, Children's Hospital Oakland Research Institute, and Juvenon, Inc.

13. *Science Daily*, source Oregon State University, 25 September 2007.
14. Fourth International Scientific Symposium on Tea & Human Health, Washington, DC, 18 September, 2007.
15. PR Newswire, 19 September 2007.
16. www.research.nottingham.ac.uk/NewsReviews/newsDisplay
17. www.liv.ac.uk/newsroom/press_releases/2006/12/shakespeare_brain.htm
18. www.ctv.ca/servlet/ArticleNews/story/CTVNews/20070112/bilingualism_dementia
19. www.uphs.upenn.edu/news/News_Releases/apr06/CSM.htm
20. *Evangelical Times*, October 2007, p. 13.

Chapter 7

1. Independent.ie/health/living-with-death-10924.html
2. 'Do not go gentle into that good night' by Dylan Thomas.
3. *Dancing with Dementia*, p. 97.
4. www.alzheimers.org.uk/VascularDementia/seminars_Penrith.htm
5. www.archpsyc.ama-assn.org/cgi/content/abstract/64/7/802
6. www.harrisinteractive.com/news/newsletters/clientnews/2006_AFA
7. www.hon.ch/News/HSN/605446.html
8. www.kcl.ac.uk/depsta/ppro/headlines/
9. Published in *Lancet Neurology*, September 2007, the development of new guidelines was co-led by Dr Howard Feldman, head of the Div. of Neurology in the University of British Columbia's Faculty of Medicine. Feldman, who directs the Clinic for Alzheimer's Disease

and Related Disorders at Vancouver Coastal Health, co-authored the paper with French researcher Dr Bruno Dubois and investigators from countries that include Japan, the US and England. Feldman is a member of Vancouver Coastal Health Research Institute (VCHRI).
10. www.seniorjournal.com/NEWS/Alzheimers/6-10-03-EarliestDetectionOfAlzheimers.htm
11. *Stroke*, July 2007.
12. www.medschool.slu.edu/agingsuccessfully/pdfsurveys/sumsexam_05.pdf
13. Bmj.com.Maguire et al.313 (7056): 529
14. Conor P. Maguire et. al., 'Family Members' Attitudes towards Telling the Patient with Alzheimer's Disease their Diagnosis', BMJ 1996:313, 529–530 C31 August. See www.bmj.com/cgi/content/ful/313/7056/529
15. *The Man Who Mistook His Wife for a Hat*, pp. 16–17.

Chapter 8

1. www.alzheimer's.org.au/upload/MediaRelease 12Sept07.pdf
2. *Dancing with Dementia*, p. 40.
3. *Dancing with Dementia*, p. 56.
4. www.dasninternational.org
5. www.womenshealthmatters.ca/resources/
6. www.dasninternational.org
7. Malcolm Goldsmith, *In a Strange Land*, Southwell: 4M Publications, 2004, p. 70.
8 Alzheimer's Association, Massachusetts Chapter Newsletter, Volume 20, No. 1, p. 14.
9. *Guardian*, Friday 25 June 2004.
10. *Daily Mail*, 3 October 2007.

11. www.timesonline.co.uk/tol/news/uk/health/article2234481.ece?token=null&offset=12
12. Phil Murran, *The Imaginary Time Bomb: Why an Ageing Population is Not a Social Problem* (I.B. Tauris & Co. Ltd., 2000).
13. www.spiked-online.com/index.php?/site/article/2915/
14. www.aafp.org/afp/981001ap/delagarz.html
15. www.health.nytimes.com/health/guides/disease/alzheimers-disease/medications.html
16. 'Developing and Implementing Local Extra Care Housing Strategies', published for the Department of Health by the Housing Learning and Improvement Network, 2002.

Chapter 9

1. www.clarksvilleonline.com/2007/08/23/caregiver-syndrome-reality
2. www.irishhealth.com/clin/alzheim/newsstory.php?id=12358
3. www.alzheimers.org.uk/Working_with_people_with_dementia/carepathways.htm
4. *Journal of Advanced Nursing*, 'Caring for a relative with dementia: family caregiver burden', Volume 58, Number 5, June 2007, pp. 446–457(12).
5. Richard Schulz and Scott Beach, *Journal of American Medical Association*, December 1999.
6. www.mindingourelders.com
7. See Minding our Elders: 'There's a hole in my soul'.
8. *Daily Express*, Saturday 13 October 2007.
9. www.parishnursing.co.uk/

Chapter 10

1. Richard Taylor, *Alzheimer's from the Inside Out* (Baltimore, MD: Health Professions Press, 2007).
2. Ngaire Beehre, 'Spiritual Care for the Frail Elderly with Alzheimer's Disease', www.sgm.org.nz
3. Jeanne Lee, *Just Love Me: My Life Turned Upside Down by Alzheimer's* (Purdue University Press, 2003).
4. *The Guardian*, October 2005.
5. Christian Council on Ageing Dementia Group, *Newsletter* 28, October 2006, p. 6.

Chapter 11

1. Charles Moore, 'Like the slave, is the unborn child not a man and a brother?', *Daily Telegraph*, 27 October 2007.
2. Head of the Bradford Dementia Group, University of Bradford.

Chapter 12

1. Jane Lapotaire, *Time Out of Mind*, London: Virago Press, 2004, zp. 301.

Chapter 13

1. www.onthemove.org.uk

The world in which Pilgrim Homes came into being in 1807 was vastly different to the one we know today. John Bunyan's book, *The Pilgrim's Progress from This World to That Which Is to Come*, first published in February 1678, was continuing to remind Christians that they were pilgrims on a journey through life to something more lasting. Pilgrimage is a Scriptural concept, mentioned throughout the Bible from the beginning of the Old Testament to the end of the New. It seems to have been in the thoughts of the Pilgrim Fathers on board the *Mayflower* when it set sail from Plymouth in September 1620. It was certainly in the minds of the group of men and women in London who, in the founding document of 12th August, 1807, named the new charity 'The Aged Pilgrims' Friend Society.' And so it proved to be.

Although the British Empire covered twenty percent of the world's landmass, conditions in Britain itself were abysmal. The poverty of post-Napoleonic war Britain was appalling, and for many only the workhouse stood between them and starvation. Although many agencies had sprung up to help the poor, none looked out specifically for elderly Christians. In his first appeal to 'the religious public,' Pilgrim Homes' founder James Bisset wrote, 'Amidst the great number of charitable institutions with which this highly favoured land abounds it is to be lamented that one numerous class of deserving person is left deserted and forsaken, namely, the aged and infirm Christian poor. There are many of this description, who after having spent a laborious life in honest poverty, and worn down with old age and bodily infirmity are, in the winter of life, shut up in garrets and cellars, lingering the remainder of their days in distress and wretchedness ... Some of these dear people of God have been found so distressed as to be literally starving with hunger, and no bed to rest their infirm limbs but a little straw on the floor, without any other covering but what their miserable clothing afforded them.' With financial help in the form of regular pensions, and gifts of coal, blankets and food, the APFS, as it became known, became a life-line to desperate 'aged pilgrims'. Along with the practical help was always spiritual support and encouragement, and from the beginning, our ministry was based on Galatians 6:10, doing good 'especially to the household of faith'.

But despite these conditions, (or perhaps, because of them), in society at large in the early 1800s there was an underlying Christian hope and, although not universally adopted, there was high regard for the Christian faith and its principles. Now, at the start of the 21st century and in times of unparalled plenty, it is almost completely the opposite. We seem to be seeing poverty of another kind, the sort of famine described by Amos in the Old Testament: 'Not a famine of bread, nor a thirst for water, but of hearing the words of the LORD.' (Amos 8:11). Our society is becoming ever more secular and humanist, and with its aggrandizement of human beings and its diminution of God, tries to extinguish Christian faith and principles. It is a difficult world for elderly Christians. Age is a time of loss – loss of a life-time of family and friends one has trusted, loss of physical and mental strength, loss of feeling a 'useful contributor', and even loss of trust in one's own judgement. In the spiritual battle the Bible tells us we are daily engaged in, the weak are given no quarter. Satan reserves his sharpest arrows for the frail elderly, and even the strongest warriors can begin to doubt their salvation. This is when loving Christian care and encouragement is so important. In each of our homes there are daily prayers and Bible readings, and mid-week and Sunday services (for those who can't attend their own churches) taken by members of local evangelical churches.

There are nine Pilgrim Homes' care schemes in different parts of the UK, offering residential and nursing care, sheltered, very sheltered housing and extra care housing. Each scheme benefits from groups of supporters, who provide friendship, spiritual encouragement and practical help, such as trips to the shops or to the doctor, or to keep a hospital appointment. Our support group structure is unique, even amongst Christian care providers, and is seen by very many, including secular authorities, as contributing invaluably to the lives of our residents, and to the atmosphere of our homes. This aspect of what we do has been recognised as providing something that our beneficiaries would not be able to access elsewhere.

Chief Executive, Peter Tervet said, 'From the outset our Society has been a work of God. It was started by God and its resources have always come from His people.' More than anything, we value prayer and, as you close this book, I'd like to take the opportunity of asking you to remember us in your prayers.

CONTACT PILGRIM HOMES

Pilgrim Homes
175 Tower Bridge Road
London
SE1 2AL
Tel: 020 7407 5466
www.pilgrimhomes.org.uk
info@pilgrimhomes.org.uk